A Bawdy Language

A Bawdy Language

How a Second-Rate Language
Slept Its Way to the Top

Howard Richler

Foreword by Richard Lederer

Published in 1999 by Stoddart Publishing Co. Limited
34 Lesmill Road, Toronto, Canada M3B 2T6
180 Varick Street, 9th Floor, New York, New York 10014

Distributed in Canada by:
General Distribution Services Ltd.
325 Humber College Boulevard, Toronto, Canada M9W 7C3
Tel. (416) 213-1919   Fax (416) 213-1917
Email customer.service@ccmailgw.genpub.com

Distributed in the United States by:
General Distribution Services Inc.
85 River Rock Drive, Suite 202, Buffalo, New York 14207
Toll-free Tel. 1-800-805-1083   Toll-free Fax 1-800-481-6207
Email gdsinc@genpub.com

03 02 01 00 99 1 2 3 4 5

Canadian Cataloguing in Publication Data

Richler, Howard, 1948–
A bawdy language: how a second-rate language slept its way to the top

ISBN 0-7737-3186-5

1. English language — History. I. Title.

PE1075.R52 1999   420'.9   C98-933085-0

Every reasonable effort has been made to contact the holders of copyright
for materials quoted in this book. The author and publisher will gladly
receive information that will enable them to rectify any inadvertent
errors or omissions in subsequent editions.

Jacket Design: Bill Douglas @ The Bang
Text Design: Tannice Goddard
Text Layout: Mary Bowness

Printed and bound in Canada

*Stoddart Publishing gratefully acknowledges the Canada Council for the Arts
and the Ontario Arts Council for their support of its publishing program.*

To Jeremy and Jennifer

Contents

Foreword

I have always thought that English is a truly intoxicating language, so I'm not surprised at the findings of scientists in India who have discovered a way to convert old newspapers into alcohol. The cellulose in the newsprint is broken down by a fungus into glucose and then fermented with yeast. Although they can't explain why, the inventors of the process have discovered that old copies of the upscale English-language daily *Hindustan Times* yield the most intoxicating results, more mind-spinning than the Indian-language newspapers.

The author of this book is an intoxicated and intoxicating wordaholic who gets unrepentantly high on all flavors, savors, bouquets, and proofs of words: a genuine, certified, authentic verbivore who feasts on words — ogles their appetizing shapes, hues, and textures, swishes them around in his mouth, lingers over their many tastes, lets their juices course down his chin. I know Howard Richler, my colleague in columny, as a user-friendly, fly-by-the-roof-of-the-mouth logolept and lexicomaniac, heels-over-head in love with the English language. What more delightful guide to take us on a joy ride through the glories and oddities of this linguistic wonder of the world, this cheerfully democratic and hospitable language, this treasure of our tongue — this English?

The rise of English as a planetary language is an unparalleled success story that begins long ago, in the middle of the fifth century A.D. At the onset of the Middle Ages, several large tribes of sea rovers, the Angles, Saxons, and Jutes, lived along the continental North Sea coast, from Denmark to Holland. Around A.D. 449, these Teutonic plunderers sailed across the water and invaded the islands then known as Britannia. They found the land pleasant and the people, fighting among themselves, very easy to conquer, so they remained there. They brought with them a Low Germanic tongue that, in its new setting, became Anglo-Saxon, or Old English, the ancestor of the English we use today. In A.D. 827, King Egbert first named Britannia *Englaland*, "land of the Angles," because the Angles were at that time the chief people there. The language came to be called *Englisc*.

From those humble beginnings has arisen the new lingua franca of science, literature, diplomacy, business, trade, and travel. English is the native tongue of about 10 percent of the world's population and the native or official language of eighty-seven countries. About one of every four people riding this planet can be reached by English in some form, and more than half — and the more rapidly growing segment — did not grow up hearing English as babies and speaking it as children. They learned English as a second or third or fourth language.

Half of all books in the world are published in English. Sixty percent of all telephone calls are made in English, with 70 percent of international mail and telexes written and addressed in English. Eighty percent of all computer text is stored in English and 82.6 percent of all home pages are cast in English.

When the spacecraft *Voyager* embarked on its immense journey to Jupiter and beyond in the late 1970s, it carried a recorded message addressed to extraterrestrial beings, beginning with a statement from the Secretary-General of the United Nations — in English. If ever our descendants make contact with articulate beings from other planets and other solar systems, English will doubtless start adding and assimilating words from Martian, Saturnian, and Alpha Centaurian and beaming its vocabulary across outer space. Then English will become a truly universal language.

RICHARD LEDERER

Introduction

On a recent trip to China, French Prime Minister Lionel Jospin stated that "the English language will be used by everyone, it will lose its original beauty, while French . . . will retain its purity." In other words, Jospin was saying that whereas the French language can be likened to a beautiful virgin, the English language should be seen as a worn-out harlot. Jospin's linguistic chauvinism notwithstanding, he's right in a certain sense. You don't get to be the global language by staying pure.

Consider the facts:

- English now has an official status in eighty-seven countries and territories, far more than any other language.
- Eighty-three percent of students in the European Union are studying English.
- Since 1989, the Pasteur Society in Paris has published three of its most important scientific journals in English.

- Of the world's roughly 12,500 international organizations, 85 percent make use of the English language, with one-third using English exclusively.
- At the headquarters of Airbus, a consortium of French, English, and Spanish companies in Toulouse, France, the working language is English.

The story of the English language is a classic rags-to-riches tale. In the year A.D. 450, following the withdrawal of Roman troops from Britain, four marauding Germanic tribes — the Angles, Frisians, Jutes, and Saxons — crossed the North Sea and overran the Celts. Fifty years later, according to Robert McCrum, William Cran, and Robert MacNeil's *The Story of English*, "Englisc, incomprehensible to modern ears, was probably spoken by about as few people as currently speak Cherokee — and with about as much influence."

With the ascension of the French-speaking Normans to the throne of England in 1066, the influence of the English language probably decreased. English remained the language of the peasantry. In fact, until the year 1399, England lacked a ruler whose mother tongue was English.

Even in the days of William Shakespeare, English was not a "world class language." In 1582, scholar Thomas Mulcaster lamented that "the English tongue is of small account, stretching no further than this island of ours, nay not there over all."

When Thomas More published *Utopia* in 1516, it was printed not in English but in Latin. At the time, French, German, Spanish, and Italian all had far more speakers than English did. Today, English has as many speakers as these four languages combined. Bill Bryson, in *The Mother Tongue*, opines that it is "a cherishable irony that a language that succeeded almost by stealth, treated for centuries as the inadequate and second-rate tongue of peasants, should one day become the most important and successful language in the world." Albert C. Baugh and

Thomas Cable, in *A History of the English Language*, state that "by making English the language mainly of uneducated people, the Norman conquest made it easier for grammatical changes to go forward unchecked."

This fluid situation in the sixteenth century allowed writers to draw beauty and power from the imperfections of the English language. One man alone coined close to two thousand new English words. His contribution is characterized by etymologist Ernest Weekly as being "ten times greater than that of any writer to any language in the history of the world." I speak of the aforementioned William Shakespeare. Shakespeare was not encumbered by a prescriptive tradition ordaining proper usage, stemming the flow of the natural rhythms of the language.

Obviously, the spread of English to the New World and the dominance of the United States in world affairs are the major, but not the only, reasons for the rise of the language to its present-day preeminence. According to Richard Lederer, author of *The Miracle of Language*, English has become dominant because of the "internationality of its words and the relative simplicity of its grammar . . . and has never rejected a word because of its race, creed, or national origin." It has accumulated its vocabulary largely because of its willingness to accept foreign words. The success of English, however, can't be attributed solely to its hospitality. English has also flourished because of its fluid nature. Robert Claiborne, in *Our Marvelous Native Tongue*, suggests: "Like any other language, English ultimately reflects the imagination and creativity of those who speak and write it, from poets and scholars to crooks and beggars. And though Anglo-American linguistic creativity is doubtless no more vigorous than that of many other peoples, it has operated with almost no inhibitions, while in other places it has too often been checked (though never blocked absolutely) by the upraised finger of official or scholarly authority." It is perhaps instructive that the English language, the first worldwide lingua franca, or common language, is the only major tongue never to have formed a protective language academy. In the first section of this book, Flexibility: The Strength of English, I will discuss aspects of the fluid nature of our language.

Perhaps the genius of the English language is to be found in its inherent chaos. In English, unlike most other languages, the natural rhythms of language are allowed to flourish. English has flourished precisely because its standards have not been entrenched. Unlike Prime Minister Jospin, I believe that English, in being "used by everybody," is beautified, not made ugly. The second section of this book, entitled Variety: The Spice of English, will explore the many ways in which multiculturalism enriches our language.

Because the English language has been so promiscuous, many of its words have lurid histories. In the segment Genealogy: The Pedigree of a Mongrel Language, we'll examine some English etymologies.

The fourth segment, entitled Instrumentality: The Use and Abuse of English, will discuss the strategies of our language. Language is used as a tool — to communicate, but also to enhance one's status. While speaking basic English may be relatively easy, mastering our language is another matter, for English is uncomplicated only at the surface level. This segment looks at such devices as euphemism, idiomatic structure, linguistic prejudices, and multiple meanings.

We shouldn't forget that our language does not operate in a vacuum. Other languages provide different perspectives on the world, and every native English-speaker would be well advised to learn about other tongues. Fully three-quarters of our words are not of Anglo-Saxon origin. In the segment Commonality: The Bedmates of English, we will explore facets of other languages.

In my final segment, entitled Jollity: The Play of English, I'll explore the sheer delight one can have playing with the words of our zany, bawdy language.

My aim in writing *A Bawdy Language* is to demonstrate why the English language is in such good shape, and to explain to the reader what he or she should know to fully enjoy the world's global language. Hop aboard for a rollicking ride.

I would like to thank certain individuals for their support: *Gazette* books editor Bryan Kemchinsky, Stoddart Publishing editor Marnie Kramarich, and most of all the "shvesters," Ruth Richler and Linda Schwartz, for the gentle firmness of their editorial suggestions.

Part One

Flexibility:
The Strength of English

Nowadays, more new words are being spawned from the world of computers than from any other sphere. In his introduction to *The New Hacker's Dictionary*, Eric S. Raymond sums up the grammatical structure of cyberspeak (which is exclusively English) with the following statements: "All nouns can be verbed" and "All verbs can be nouned." Thus we can use expressions such as *mouse it up* and *winnitude*. In other words, anything goes.

In "non-cyber" domains, word formation is not quite this carefree; nevertheless, there exists in the English language a liberal attitude to neologisms. In these chapters, we'll discuss the ingenious techniques employed to form new words.

1

And the word of the year is . . .

"*E*arlier that day, Jim bemoaned having a *bad hair day* while *inline skating*, and by nightfall he was lucky not to be a *flatliner*."

"While *channel surfing* the science stations, she caught glimpses of shows on the following subjects: *biodiversity*, *artificial reality*, *cold fusion*, and *ozone-friendly* chemicals."

At the turn of the decade, these two statements would have been totally incomprehensible to most people. All the italicized words are neologisms drawn from *The Barnhart Dictionary Companion* from 1991 to 1993.

In *Fifty Years Among the New Words*, John Algeo says that as people change "through invention, discovery, revolution, evolution or personal transformation, so does their language. Like the growth rings around a tree, our vocabulary bears witness to our past." According to *Webster's Ninth New College Dictionary*, the year I was born, 1948, also featured the genesis of the words *automation* and *slap shot*; my son's birth year, 1975, featured *heavy metal* and *retrovirus*; and my daughter's birth year, 1978, featured *pro-life* and *triathlete*. Of course, not all new terms are equally memorable. From Algeo's 1976 entries we have the eminently forgettable *beefalo* and *cliometrician*.

Each year, the Academy of Motion Picture Arts and Sciences honors the year's memorable movies. Word-lovers will be happy to know that, since the beginning of this decade, the American Dialect Society has been having its own award night to honor its passion — namely, words and phrases.

So without any further ado, let me announce the five nominees for 1997 Word of the Year.

A) *duh*
B) *jitterati*
C) *millennium bug*
D) *-(r)azzi*
E) *road rage*
(The winner will be announced at the end of the chapter.)

According to the rules of the Society, "words or phrases do not have to be brand new, since few completely new words attain wide currency, but they do have to be newly prominent or distinctive. The selection is serious, based on members' tracking of new words during the year, but it is far from solemn, since many of the words represent fads and foibles of the year."

Here are the previous honorees:

1990 *bushlips* (insincere political rhetoric)
1991 *mother-of-all* (greatest, most impressive)
1992 *not!* (expression of disagreement)
1993 *information superhighway* (network linking various electronic means of communication)
1994 (tie) *cyber* (pertaining to computers) and *morph* (to change forms)

1995 (tie) *world wide web* and *newt* (to make aggressive changes as a newcomer)

1996 *soccer mom* (newly significant type of voter)

Interestingly, the two neologisms that have not endured are the two with American political connotations, *bushlips* and *newt*. It is too early to judge whether the other political candidate, *soccer mom*, will have more staying power.

Just as the Academy of Motion Pictures offers awards in categories other than Best Movie, the Society also honors words that have attained distinction in a particular field. Here's a sampling:

Most Euphemistic: (1997) *exit bag* (bag placed over the head to assist in suicide); (1996) *urban camping* (living homeless in a city); (1994) *challenged* (indicating an undesirable or unappealing condition).

Most Unnecessary: (1997) *heaven-o* (replacement for the greeting hello, approved by the God-fearing city council of Kingsville, Texas); (1996) *Mexican hustle* (alternate name for the macarena); (1992) *gender feminism* (the belief that sex roles are social, not biological).

Most Outrageous: (1997) *Florida flambé* (fire caused by Florida electric chair); (1996) *toy soldier* (land mine); (1995) *starter marriage* (a first marriage not expected to last); (1992) *ethnic cleansing*; (1990) *politically correct*. Here it is interesting to note that while *ethnic cleansing* and *politically correct* were deemed "outrageous," they have nonetheless endured.

Other miscellaneous winners of note include 1993's winners *cybersex* and *Mcjob*, in the categories of "most amazing" and "most imaginative" respectively, and the 1996 winner for "most controversial" word, *Ebonics*.

And now to 1997's Word of the Year. The fourth runner-up is the word *duh*, an expression for stupidity. Tied for third place are *jitterati* and *road rage*. The former is a word to describe coffee fetishists; the latter refers to the anger drivers feel toward their fellow motorists.

The final vote was close: *-(r)azzi*, a suffix denoting an aggressive pursuer of a specified kind, as in "stalkerazzi" or "paparazzi," received fifteen votes. This, however, was exceeded by the 1997 Word of the Year, *millennium bug*, which received twenty-one votes. *Millennium bug* is the program that causes older computer software to compute the year after 1999 as 1900. This has the potential to create massive computer failures when we reach the year 2000. *The Globe and Mail* highlighted this problem in its February 4, 1998, headline, which read "Year 2000 Crackdown Urged." Its text stated that "the Conference Board of Canada warned that failure to deal immediately with the millennium bug could throw Canada into a recession in the first half of 2000 and derail the country's progress to full employment by 2001."

And you thought national unity was Canada's biggest crisis? Duh!

P.S. This book will go to press too early to include 1998's Word of the Year. My leading candidate? Viagra.

2

Marathon running into another century

*Q*uestion: What do the words *genocide, cosmonaut,* and *cyberhate* have in common? Answer: They are all words that have filtered into the English language since the end of World War II thanks to suffixes and prefixes.

The horrors of the 1940s gave us *genocide,* derived by combining the prefix *genoa* (many people) with the suffix *-cide* (killing). The race to the moon between the United States and the Soviet Union necessitated competing vocabulary. Thus was born the term *cosmonaut* (literally, a sailor of the cosmos) to refer to Russians who performed the same function as American *astronauts.* The *cyber* prefix in *cyberhate* descends ultimately from the Greek *kybernetes,* meaning "steersman." Although *cyberhate* is not to be found in dictionaries, its sense is clear, as in this recent statement by a B'nai B'rith of Canada official: "We are witnessing an exponential growth in cyberhate." *Cyber* has become the prefix of choice to describe computers.

It is routine for prefixes and suffixes to develop new senses. For example, the *agri* in "agriculture" technically means "field," but when it is used in a word such as *agribusiness*, it takes on the sense of the whole word agriculture. Similarly, the -*genic* suffix in "photogenic" means "produced by." But as the sense of photogenic shifted to mean "good as a subject of photography," the meaning of the suffix -*genic* shifted likewise in words such as *telegenic* and *mediagenic*.

The Oxford Companion to the English Language states that "new words are often the subject of scorn . . . because they are perceived as unaesthetically or improperly formed." The bête noire for linguistic prescriptivists is the word *telethon*. At one point, *The Oxford English Dictionary* characterized it as "barbarously extracted from marathon, used occasionally in the U.S., rarely in Britain."

To trace the roots of *telethon*, let us return to 490 B.C. In this year, the Greeks defeated the Persians at Marathon and a runner was dispatched thence to bring the good tidings to Athens. In the inaugural modern-day Olympics held in Athens in 1896, this grueling 26-mile and 385-yard run was reenacted, and so the word *marathon* entered the lexicon.

Marathons were soon to escape the Olympic arena into less athletic, albeit just as grueling, events. There is a citation in *The Oxford English Dictionary* from the *Daily Chronicle* in 1908 which states that "[a] competition under the title 'the Murphy Marathon' was decided last night. . . . It was intended that the contestants should peel a quarter of a hundredweight of potatoes."

Then, in 1949, our "barbarism" was at last unleashed. The *San Francisco Examiner* reported on a "telethon" held between April 22 and April 25 to raise money. At least the newspaper had the delicacy to put its Frankenstein of a word in quotation marks to indicate that it was a neologism. *Telethon* was to endure, and it gained respectability when it was recorded in the *Oxford English Dictionary Supplement*, Volume 4 (1986). It was defined as a "TV program lasting several hours, especially to solicit contributions," coined by analogy from "marathon." Alas, a false analysis had unraveled "marathon" into two dubious morphemes, *mar(a)* now meant "running," and *thon* now meant "long."

Words that have distinctive endings are particularly subject to this mutation. The Watergate affair gets its name from the office complex that housed the headquarters of the burglarized Democratic National Committee. The *-gate* suffix to refer to a scandal, however, is used so pervasively that I'm sure most people think *billingsgate* refers to a Medicare scam. (It actually means "coarsely abusive language.")

A similar situation exists with the suffix *-holic* to refer to a person with a compulsive need. An alcoholic is not addicted to "alco" but to "alcohol." Therefore, the *-holic* suffix is technically meaningless. Nevertheless, the nouns used to designate many *holic* compulsions, such as *workaholic*, are to be found in dictionaries, or at least recognized by the average chocolate-craver on the streets (i.e., *chocoholic*). Unlike the case of *billingsgate*, however, most people realize that a *Catholic* is not addicted to cats.

Although a distinctive ending, such as *-thon* or *-gate*, is conducive to a suffix taking on a distinct, albeit grammatically incorrect meaning, it is not an absolute necessity. Witness the more plebeian *-icize* and *-ercise* endings featured in such words as *anglicize*, *criticize*, and *cauterize*. "Physical fitness-holics" have absconded with these endings with terms such as *jazzercize*, *dancercise*, *aerobicize*, and *sexercize*, all modeled on the word *exercise*. While the operative activity in all these neologisms is dancing, in the case of *sexercize* it is limited to the horizontal rumba.

3

Words are blending in all over

*W*hat do *televangelist, tangelo,* and *Spam* have in common?

All these words are blends, words formed by fusing elements of two other words. The elements are normally the beginning of one word and the end of another. Thus "television" and "evangelist" provide *televangelist,* "tangerine" and "pomelo" yield *tangelo,* and Hormel Foods gave us *Spam* in 1937 by blending "spiced" and "ham."

Lewis Carroll dubbed such words portmanteaus. He loved to scrunch words together into one word and thought this process was similar to cramming clothes into a travelling bag, which is also known as a portmanteau.

The most famous example of Carroll's blending ability is to be found in his "Jabberwocky" poem in *Through the Looking Glass*. It begins as follows:

'Twas brillig, and the slithy toves
Did gyre and gimble in the wabe;
All mimsy were the borogoves,
And the mome raths outgrabe.

Humpty Dumpty explains to Alice that "slithy" means lithe and slimy. "You see, it's like a portmanteau — there are two meanings packed up in one word; and mimsy is flimsy and miserable." Carroll's portmanteaus were nonce words, invented for use on only one occasion, but two words that appear later in the "Jabberwocky" poem have endured and are enshrined in English-language dictionaries. I refer to *chortle*, a blend of "chuckle" and "snort," and *galumph*, a combo of "gallop" and "triumph."

Before Carroll wrote *Through the Looking Glass* in 1871, the formation of blended words was quite rare. *Anecdotage* was coined in 1823, and it combined "anecdote" and "dotage" to suggest the proclivity to tell stories in one's senior years. The blend *squirl* came into being in 1843. It combined "squiggle" and "whirl" to describe a handwriting characterized by great flourishes. In 1849 Herman Melville coined the derisive term *snivelization*, blending "snivel" with "civilization." Jane Austen used the term *mizzle* in *Emma*, written in 1816. It was a blend of "mist" and "drizzle." Sixteenth-century writers Edmund Spenser and William Shakespeare respectively employed *wrizzled*, a blend of "wrinkled" and "frizzled," and *glaze*, a blend of "glare" and "gaze."

Probably influenced by Carroll's portmanteaus, blending words became the rage near the end of the century. *Electrocute* was formed in 1889 by blending "electricity" and "execute"; *prissy* blended "prim" and "sissy" in 1895; *brunch* blended "breakfast" and "lunch" in 1896; and *motel* was born in 1925 by blending "motor" with "hotel."

Language writer Michael Quinion states that a distinction should be maintained between blends and compound words, such as *keypad*, *townhouse*, and *teletext*. The latter are composed of words in their own right, or created by adding recognizable prefixes and suffixes. This dichotomy can be fuzzy, however, particularly when certain suffixes are involved. *Motorcade* was a blend of "motor" and "cavalcade," and *telethon* was a blend of "television" and "marathon." But the suffixes *-cade* and *-thon* have taken on such definable meanings that terms such as *aerocade* or *dancethon* have to be considered compounds and not blends.

Blends are very popular as names for slogans and concepts. Some examples of this are *cocacolonization*, *Reagonomics*, *squattocracy*, and *californicate*. *Squattocracy* was a sarcastic term used in nineteenth-century Australia that blended "squatter" and "aristocracy." It mocked squatters who had acquired great wealth. The verb *californicate* is an American usage that has come to refer to using one state's policy in another state. The slogan "Don't Californicate Oregon" has become a rallying cry in the Pacific Northwest. Blends are also very popular in referring to the commingling of languages — observe *Yinglish*, *Spanglish*, *Japlish*, *Taglish* (Tagalog and English), *Malenglish* (Malay and English), *slanguage*, and *Franglais*.

Sniglets, "words that don't exist, but should," often blend words. Some examples of this genre are: *phonesia*, the affliction of dialing a phone number and forgetting whom you were calling when someone answers; *telecrastination*, the act of letting the phone ring at least twice, even when you're only six inches away; and *excrementality*, the waste of a mind.

Blends are also used in the animal kingdom. You'll find a *liger* and a *tigon* listed in dictionaries, the former being the progeny of a lion and tigress and the latter being the result of the union of a tiger and lioness. I have seen references to the following mutant forms: *chimpanutang*, *orangorilla*, and *yow* (yak and cow). Thankfully none of these blends has as yet received lexicographic recognition.

Nor has the progeny of a pheasant and a duck which would be . . . a *deasant*, of course.

4

Slang ain't so bad

*F*or those who think all dictionaries avoid value judgments in their definitions, I suggest a reading of the entry in *The Oxford English Dictionary* (2nd edition) (OED) under the headword "slang." The OED defines slang as "the special vocabulary used by any set of persons of a low or disreputable character; language of a low and vulgar type."

To which I say, thank God for disreputable characters.

Without slang there might be linguistic stagnation. It was the slangy Latin of Plautus and Petronius that "corrupted" the classical language of Horace and Cicero. Had Latin not been corrupted, the French works of Molière, Italian works of Dante, and Spanish works of Cervantes might have been written in Latin. Had Middle English not been tampered with, we would not now enjoy the majesty of Shakespeare.

The word *slang* is first used in the English language in the middle of the eighteenth century. Its etymology is either from an improper use of the past tense of the verb "sling," or the combination of a term like "thieves' language" or "hoboes' language." As it was originally used, the word referred to the special vocabulary of a particular group. Often the group in question would be seen as "shady" by genteel society. Slang in its infancy had the connotation of abusive language, as in "slanging match." In Scotland and the north of England, the term slang still refers to abusive as opposed to sub-standard language.

Nowadays, it is difficult to pin down the nature of slang. As Phillip Howard puts it in *The State of the Language*, "one man's slang is another man's colloquialism is another man's vernacular is another man's everyday speech." Slang is usually seen as being more transitory and more picturesque than standard language.

It is becoming a problem in English now to declare what is "standard." I've heard many people lament that words like *gay* and *grass* have ended up in a *slang heap*. Actually, the opposite tendency is more common. Many slang words lose their slang status and get promoted into standard language. For example, the words *sandwich*, *dwindle*, *slump*, *bellhop*, *spurious*, *quiz*, *jeopardy*, *crestfallen*, and *mob* were all once lowly, and often vilified, slang words.

Although condemned by purists as a bastardization of language, slang is a monument to the ability of language to evolve. By cutting through its euphemistic and pretentious nature, slang refreshes language by supplying substitutes for words that have grown weary. Over time, too much linguistic familiarity breeds listlessness. Slang is a response to our need for variety.

Slang terms are constantly in a state of flux. New words are always required for words that are no longer in fashion. Only occasionally will slang words live long in their protean world. Two examples of long-enduring slang terms, however, are *bones*, to mean "dice," and the phrase *beat it*. Chaucer used *bones* in its present-day gambling context, and Shakespeare employed the expression *beat it* in a slangish mode.

The function of slang is that it becomes a badge for a group. It adds to the group's sense of solidarity by supplying a code that helps distinguish members from non-members. Having a lingo that is not known outside of the group enhances the group's sense of being special.

Slang is used and created much more by males than by females. Males seem to revel in slang's ability to shock. According to the *Dictionary of Slang*, edited by J. S. Farmer and W. E. Henley, "[g]irls generally learn the standard, even the technical, words before they learn the slang that the boys, contrariwise, take in with every association."

Since slang is the language of the "now," I've prepared a little test to check out your "cool" quotient. Do you "dig" the following quote I found on the Internet? "Some people wrote that *speed garage* is just *handbag house* with just few things changed. Well I say a little change goes a lot further than that and change one or two elements in *house* and you can make a *house* into *techno* if you want."

If you don't understand it, it is because you are not conversant in the arcane argot of "clubspeak." Montreal music maven Mireille Silcott recently initiated me into the rudiments of this lingo by sharing with me some of the terms that have recently been spawned by club culture.

For example, many disc jockeys have evolved into *turntablists*. According to a job description I read on the Web, a *turntablist* "creates out of cords, two turntables, a mixer, new music techniques including scratchin', backspins, cuts, etc."

If you're curious to know what the italicized words in my slang paragraph mean, this is the Standard English explanation provided by Silcott. "In the early '80s, a bunch of DJs in Chicago took the vocal out of disco, quickened the pace and bolstered the bass, and it was named 'house music'. . . . A bit earlier on in New York . . . a DJ named Larry Levan was doing the same thing, only leaving the vocals in. Levan's style was slower than the

Chicago style. Levan's sound was called 'garage' and later, 'garage house.'"

Silcott explains that *speed garage* is a subgenre developed in the United Kingdom "which runs at about 140 beats per minute (faster than most house genres), and relies on sped-up four-on-the-floor beat." British dance magazines coined the term, and it quickly moved into the public domain. *Handbag house* is "the kind of dance music that appeals to cheesy girls — the type who leave their purses on the dance floor and dance near them." *Techno*, she relates, was developed in Detroit circa 1989, and it is a "colder, harder house."

According to *The Oxford Companion to the English Language* (OCEL), the "slang vocabulary of a language is ephemeral, bursting into existence and falling out of use at a much more rapid rate than terms in the general vocabulary." "Clubspeak," Silcott says, displays this "lexical hyperspeed." For example, "even though speed garage is barely a year old, it has already spawned a ton of titled subgenres, like 'raggage' (a marriage of reggae and garage), 'street garage' and 'UK garage' (a broad style — this is becoming the umbrella term, it's replacing 'speed garage')."

The British, states Silcott, are the "most unbelievably lickety-split bunch when it comes to coming up with obscure genres and plonking dissective names on styles, sub-styles and sub-sub styles." A few of these are *acid house* ("house with squelchy noises in it"), *trip-hop* ("hip-hop mainly by white people — often with female vocals"), *trance* ("trancy, swooshy techno"), and *drill 'n' bass*, which is available in the following flavors, *hard*, *deep*, *tribal*, and *intelligent*.

British musician Paul Chambers commented recently on this stylistic proliferation. "Everyone's got their own terminology, I just make garage music. If I do come up with a definitive name, I'll get it copyrighted right away. One reason people are quick to give it a name is that if you want to take it to America, you have to give it a name, that's how they work. They have to have it categorized and pigeonholed or they can't market it."

The OCEL states that slang is used "by people who have reason to hide from people in authority what they know or do." Club culture features some coded words related to drug use that may fall into this category. There is the term *caning* (possibly a derivative of the word "cocaine"), which refers to a high intake of drugs, and the expression *sorted*, which designates a high level of satiation, usually drug-induced. The term *ecstasy*, or *E*, is a code word for the drug MDMA, but this term has been in circulation for quite a while now, so that it can no longer be considered a shibboleth.

A caveat is in order if I have inspired you to join the club scene. "Nothing is more damaging," warns the OCEL, "to status in the group than using old slang." Silcott concurs, saying that one should never refer to the drug *ecstasy* as "X" or spell it "XTC." Such usage will pigeonhole you as "a parent trying to be hip" or as "a writer for a daily newspaper who does scare stories about recreational drugs." Equally distasteful is referring to a DJ's activity as *spinning* (more proper is *mixing* or *playing*). And don't call turntables *wheels*. Silcott explains that this term "was quite big during the beginning of hip hop," but isn't any longer. Also, since rave "went commercial" in the early '90s, it has become uncool to use the phrase *on one* to refer to being *in a groove*.

Treasure slang's richness and diversity. Steven Pinker, author of *The Language Instinct*, puts it this way: "Some people worry that slang will somehow 'corrupt' the language. We should be so lucky. Most slang lexicons are preciously guarded by their subcultures as membership badges. When given a glimpse into one of these lexicons, no true language lover can fail to be dazzled by the brilliant wordplay and wit: from medical students (Zorrobelly, crispy critter, prune), rappers (jaw-jacking, dissing) . . . and hackers (to flame, core-dump, crufty). When the more passé terms get cast off and handed down to the mainstream, they often fill expressive gaps in the language beautifully."

5

Purity had nothing to do with it

*I*n 1635, L'Académie Française was established under the auspices of Cardinal Richelieu. Its mandate was "to labour with all possible care and diligence to give definite rules to [the French] language and to render it pure, eloquent and capable of treating the arts and sciences."

How well has it fulfilled its mandate? Well, it certainly has established definite rules, ossified though they may be. And no one can claim that French is not eloquent or capable of treating the arts and sciences. L'Académie, however, has not rendered French "pure." To have done so, one would have to have performed linguistic alchemy. The notion of pristine languages is as fictitious as the concept of distinct races. The French word for language, *langue*, takes the feminine gender, and if the truth be known, the lady was never pure.

Languages, like people, are promiscuous and become impregnated with foreign elements. The very name "France" informs us that the original Frenchmen were Franks, a Germanic tribe. Essentially, French and all the other Romance languages are mutated Latin that the Germanic tribes adapted from the conquering Romans. Robert Claiborne, in *The Roots of Language*, points out that "French was long ago 'corrupted' by borrowings from Gaulic (a Celtic language) and Germanic and later Italian, Spanish and Arabic. Ironically, many of the 'corruptions' are English words previously borrowed from French." Adulterations such as *rosbif*, *tennis*, *parquez*, and *stop* were originally French words, smuggled into England centuries ago.

In a work published in 1964, Professor Réné Etiemble brought the word "franglais" — a hybrid of *français* and *anglais* — into popular use. He predicted that, unless draconian measures were adopted, the French language would not last the millennium. Soon thereafter, L'Académie Française heard this clarion call and prepared lists of words and phrases that were deemed *impropre à la langue*.

This idea that French might somehow vanish is an oft-repeated one. In defense of legislation to eliminate anglicisms, French culture minister Jacques Toubon stated in 1994 that the law is "not an attack on English. It is an attempt to preserve this language, this irreplaceable capital. If it is not preserved, it will die." The literary editor of *Le Figaro*, Jean-Marie Rouart, continued in this apocalyptic tone. He stated that "the French language is a masterpiece, yet it is a masterpiece in peril," the enemy being pernicious anglicisms.

Of course the French are not alone in decrying the pollution of their tongue by English. Robert Claiborne, in *Our Marvelous Native Tongue*, relates that in the mid-1970s, Soviet journalist Vladimir Vasilyev wrote an article deploring how the Russian language had become polluted by the adoption of anglicisms such as *boss*, *referee*, *offis*, *servis*, and *plantsiya* (plantation). Ironically, none of these words is "pure" English. *Boss* comes from Dutch, *referee*, *office*, and *service* from French, and *plantation* from Latin.

And so to Messieurs Etiemble, Toubon, and Rouart and Comrade Vasilyev, I say — horsefeathers. Claiborne relates that "if borrowing foreign words could destroy a language, English would be dead (borrowed from Old Norse), deceased (from French), defunct (from Latin) and kaput (from German)." French novelist Jean D'Ormesson states that "[b]orrowed words have always enriched the language. We have accepted good foreign words like sofa and opera."

As a Canadian living in the province of Quebec, however, I am no stranger to such linguistic silliness. On October 30, 1995, a referendum was held to decide the political fate of Quebec in Canada. Quebec's deputy premier, Bernard Landry, was in a foul mood, having found himself, a separatist, on the losing side of the vote. Then, a Mexican-born hotel clerk, speaking to Monsieur Landry in French, made the mistake of asking him if he wanted to "check in," and Landry became apoplectic. Later, he justified his rage to the English media, explaining, "In Quebec, we insist on using, all the time, *enregistrer*." Hogwash. Who is to say what is a French word and what is not? Take the following list of "English" words and terms: *bon viveur, double entendre, legerdemain, nom de plume,* and *R.S.V.P.* Since none of them is to be found in a French dictionary, I suppose Landry would condemn the use of any of these dreaded anglicisms by a francophone, though each of them originates in French.

Commencing with the Norman invasion of England in 1066, French words have greatly enhanced the English vocabulary. Think how much poorer English would be without *symphony, gazette,* and *brunette.* Writer Jonathan Swift fought, in vain, against these seventeenth-century neologisms.

What's wrong if French, whose vocabulary is much smaller than that of English, borrows some useful terms? In borrowing from other languages, a language gains nuances of meaning. Often, the borrowed expression is acculturated with a distinct spelling. Increasingly, I have seen bagel rendered as *baguel* in

French. A word may even take on a particular connotation in its new linguistic environment. Take the word *chum*. In English, the word means simply "friend." In Quebec French (which sometimes uses the variant spelling *tchomme*), it has a sense somewhere in between the sophomoric-sounding "boyfriend" or "girlfriend" and the more blatant "lover."

The question of whether change is good or bad for a language is largely irrelevant. Just as species evolve and societies change, all languages are in a constant state of flux. Legislators who try to avoid inevitable change are wasting their time and the taxpayers' money. As William Safire said, "In the end democracy, which goes by the name of common usage, will work its will."

Claiborne says that "for centuries . . . English-speaking peoples have plundered the world for words" and the nice thing about this form of larceny is that "it enriches the perpetrator without impoverishing the victim."

Educator Joseph Bellafiore characterized the English language as "the lagoon of nations" because of the many words "floating like ships from foreign ports freighted with messages from us." Because of this welcoming tendency, English has accumulated by far the world's largest vocabulary — more than double the words of its nearest competitors, German, French, and Russian. Claiborne believes this gives English "the most variegated and most expressive vocabulary in the world."

Fewer than 30 percent of English words stem from the original Anglo-Saxon word stock. William Safire wrote in 1996 in his "On Language" column: "With all its grammatical irregularity and illogical pronunciation, English is best suited to be the world's bridge tongue. Why? One reason is that it's the most welcoming, absorbent, easily adaptable language in the world."

Let's examine our foreign bounty. Many of the borrowings have been in our language for such a long time that they no longer seem exotic. From Old Norse, we have the words *skirt* and *kindle*; from Latin, *wine* and *vocabulary*; from the Greek, *lexicon* and *bishop*.

In his book *Miracle of Language*, Richard Lederer lists fifty familiar English words that come from fifty different languages. For example, from thirteenth-century Sanskrit we have *sugar*; from seventeenth-century Arabic and Malay, we have *alcohol* and *ketchup* respectively; and the year 1925 yielded *boondocks* from Tagalog and *kibitzer* from Yiddish.

Only five of Lederer's fifty foreign words are from the twentieth century, and the latest one, *jukebox*, from Gullah, joined our lexicon in 1939. This is not to say, however, that we are not devouring new foreign words in this century. For example, between 1930 and 1950 alone, all these food words joined our language: *burrito*, *calzone*, *capelleti*, *feta*, *linguine*, *manicotti*, *moussaka*, *pesto*, *souvlaki*, *taco*, *tempura*, and *won ton*.

The worlds of war and international politics have also presented us with new words in this century. We have *détente* from French; *blitz* and *realpolitik* from German; *kamikaze* from Japanese; *apartheid* from Afrikaans; *glasnost* and *perestroika* from Russian; and *intifada* from Arabic.

Words that we take from other languages often acquire extended meanings in their English environs. The word *karma* in Sanskrit means "fate." In English, it has acquired the sense of "an aura of good or bad emanating from a person." Similarly, the word *blitz* (from *blitzkrieg*), which referred in World War II to a "sudden overpowering bombardment," acquired an additional sense in the 1960s when it surfaced as a term in football. *Honcho* in Japanese means "squad leader." In English, it has acquired the sense of "boss" and is starting to be used as a verb meaning "to oversee." Increasingly, I hear the German-bred noun *angst* being rendered, verb-like, in the form of *angsting*.

There are still foreign words ripe for English appropriation. Take the Yiddish word *nakhes*, which Leo Rosten, author of *The Joys of Yiddish*, defines as "proud pleasure; special joy —

particularly from the achievements of a child." English does not have a word that conveys this feeling. Howard Rheingold, in *They Have a Word for It*, lobbies for the inclusion of the Japanese word *wabi*, which he defines as "a flawed detail that creates an elegant whole."

So the next time you hear some linguistic chauvinist whine about the corruption of his language, hit him with this quote from poet Carl Sandburg: "The English language hasn't got where it is by being pure."

6

Words, words, words – Roget has them all

*W*ith its vast vocabulary, drawn from all the world's great languages, it's hardly surprising that the English language possesses an abundance of possible synonyms, giving English the potential for greater nuances of meaning than are available in other languages.

The multitudinous word choices that English offers, however, have exasperated many a non-native speaker. William Styron, in *Sophie's Choice*, highlights this in the following memorable passage, in which the heroine, Polish-born Sophie, expresses mock-horror at the variety of English words:

"Such a language! . . . Too many words. I mean just the word for *velocité*. I mean 'fast.' 'Rapid.' 'Quick.' All the same thing! A scandal."

"Swift?" I added.

"How about 'speedy'?" Nathan said.

"Hasty?" I went on.

"And fleet?" Nathan said. "Though that's a bit fancy."

"Snappy!?" I said.

"Stop it!" Sophie said, laughing. "Too much! Too many words, this English. In French it is so simple, you just say '*vite*.'"

A cartoon in *The New Yorker* in the late 1980s makes a similar point. With a caption reading "Roget's Brontosaurus," it features a big dinosaur whose thought-bubble offers: "large, great, huge, considerable, bulky, voluminous, ample, massive, capacious, spacious, mighty, towering, monstrous . . ." Not to mention "humongous," "whopping," etc., which wouldn't fit because of bubble constraints.

Simultaneous borrowing from French and Latin has created a hallmark of English vocabulary: triplets of words that are stylistically different but that convey the same approximate meaning.

Take the following trinity of synonyms drawn from Old English, French, and Latin.

Old English	French	Latin
kingly	royal	regal
ask	question	interrogate
fast	firm	secure
rise	mount	ascend
holy	sacred	consecrated
time	age	epoch

There is a tendency for the popular word to have an Old English root, with the French-based word being the literary word, and the Latin-based word being the learned option.

The varied English vocabulary presents quite a challenge when selecting the right word for the occasion. Fortunately, the publishing house Longman helped ease this problem almost one hundred and fifty years ago. In 1852, it released a reference work whose mission was "to supply, with respect to the English language, a desideratum hitherto unsupplied in any language; namely, a collection of the words it contains and of the idiomatic combinations peculiar to it, arranged, not in alphabetical order, as they are in the dictionary, but according to the ideas they express."

This reference work turned the dictionary on its head. Instead of defining a word, the book presents an idea, and then aims to find the appropriate word or words "by which that idea may be most fitly and aptly expressed."

I speak, of course, of Roget's *Thesaurus of English Words and Phrases*, written by physician-librarian Peter Mark Roget. Roget borrowed the word *thesaurus* from the field of archaeology, where it referred to the treasures of a temple. In his schema, the temple became the mind and its contents were word knowledge.

The *Thesaurus* has been revised countless times and has sold over thirty million copies worldwide in different editions. *The Oxford Companion to the English Language* says that "the words in Roget are arranged in listed sets like the genera and species of biology. The intention has not been to define or discriminate them, but to arrange them in synonymous and anonymous groups; it serves as both a word-finder and a prompter of the memory regarding words one knows but could not recall to mind."

I referred earlier to the "multitudinous word choices" of English vocabulary. According to Roget, "multitudinous" could have been replaced by *many, several, numerous, profuse, manifold*, etc. And if Sophie had not interrupted Nathan and Stingo in Styron's passage, they might have included *full-drive, precipitate, winged*, and *mercurial*.

Proper communication depends on using words correctly. Linguist S. I. Hayakawa stated that "to choose a word well is to give both illumination and delight." Or, as an anonymous civil servant phrased it, "The search for the *mot juste* is not a pedantic fad but a vital necessity. Words are our precision tools. Imprecision engenders ambiguity and hours are wasted in removing verbal misunderstanding before the argument of substance can begin."

7

Obsolete words are gone but not forgotten

*W*hich of the following two sentences, featuring italicized words, is obscene?

A) When he was a *piss-prophet* he was a *shittle fartles*, but now that he makes *spiss pissabed* wine he is generally regarded as *geason* and by no means *unpregnant*.

B) The *bronstrops* inquired whether the *franion* would like to *smick* and *halch* a *tentiginous thuften*, but he refused because he had no desire to commit *eaubruche* against his *muskin* with a *drossell*.

The correct answer is B.

The first sentence relates that a man who earned his living diagnosing urine samples (*piss-prophet*) was an unstable, trouble-some person (*shittle fartles*), but now that he has switched careers and is making thick dandelion (*spiss pissabed*) wine, he is considered to be a wonderful (*geason*) man and by no means inept at business (*unpregnant*).

Our seemingly innocuous second tale has a prostitute (*bronstrops*) approach a ladies' man (*franion*) and try to entice him to kiss and embrace a lusty maiden (*smick* and *halch* a *tentiginous thuften*). He refuses because he doesn't want to commit adultery against his sweetheart with a slut (*eaubruche* against his *muskin* with a *drossell*).

The italicized words are absent from most dictionaries. They can all, however, be found in *The Oxford English Dictionary* (OED), followed by the notation "obs.," the lexicographic abbreviation for obsolete (not obscene). The OED records all words that have graced the English language for the last thousand years. Language is in perpetual flux. Words are being continuously born, their meanings mutate as society changes, and inevitably some words die. Why? By and large it's a process of "use it or lose it."

Just as sifting through shards can tell us much about the customs of past civilizations, examining archaic words informs us about the concerns of our ancestors. For example, many of the words used in the sixteenth century that are now obsolete exhibit a passion for wordplay. Shakespeare and his peers had twenty-one words to describe today's much besmirched "pun." Among them are the now defunct *bull, liripoop, pundigrion, quiblin,* and *quarterquibble.* And then there is *floccinaucinihilipilification,* which is an estimation of an object with regard to its worthlessness. It uses four Latin words, *flocci, nauci, nihili,* and *pili,* all of which mean "at nothing," to get its point across. By the eighteenth century, however, the staid dictates of the Age of Reason ordained that such verbal flights of fancy were not altogether seemly, and many of these words faded from use.

Often words become obsolete because customs and beliefs change. Today, we survive without either a *titivil* or a *taisch*, the former being a devil who steals words dropped during recitation and the latter being an apparition of someone who is about to die. We no longer have the word *corsned* (Old English *cor*, "trial," and *snaed*, "piece") because we no longer determine guilt by observing whether an individual convulses after eating holy bread. We have lost the *bridelope* wedding custom, whereby the rushing groom would literally gallop with his blushing bride to their new home following the ceremony. And gone are the days when a *zopissa* (a medicinal application of wax and pitch) would be considered likely to soothe an *agrum* (a nasty swelling of the mouth and cheeks).

For those who see the distant past as a kinder, gentler age, I suggest an examination of some of its archaic vocabulary. We had the word *fearbabe*, for example, the term for an object whose sole function was to frighten babies. And then we had the myriad words to describe the varieties of maiming and killing. Lost to the English language are the following torturous words.

Abacinate: to blind by placing hot irons in front of the eyes.

Artuate: to divide by joints, to quarter, to dismember.

Cyphonism: punishment by pillory where one is suspended by the neck.

Elinguate: to deprive of the tongue.

Eluscate: to blind in one eye.

Excarnificate: to tear to pieces.

Scaphism: confinement in a trough with one's head dabbed with honey while exposed to the sun and varied insects.

Scarpines: an instrument of torture for the feet.

Suspercollate: to hang. According to the *Oxford English Dictionary* it derives from the Latin phrase *suspendatur per collum*, "let him be hanged by the neck."

Commencing with the Norman invasion of 1066, the status language in England was French rather than English. By the thirteenth century, however, the francophone upper classes became assimilated and, as a result, gallicisms in the English language decreased. Among those lost were the words *bellibonne*, a corrupted term for a lovely maiden derived from *belle et bonne*, "fair and good," and *male journey*, from the Old French *male journée*, "evil day," which referred to an unfortunate battle. One word I'd like to see revived is the inscrutable *chantepleure*, "to sing and cry concurrently."

Part Two

Variety:
The Spice of English

The Oxford Companion to the English Language lists over four hundred variants of our native tongue, including: Afrikaans, Australian, Botswanan, Chinook Jargon, Falkland Islands, Gibraltar, Jamaican Creole, Ottawa Valley, Pennsylvania Dutch, Tok Pisin, and Yinglish. The country with the largest number of English-speakers, the United States, represents only 20 percent of English-speakers in the world.

In each of the varieties of English, there are usages that are not comprehensible to English-speakers in other regions. In a sense, then, the term "English language" is a misnomer and should be replaced by the term "English languages." Even within the bounds of a particular variety of English, there is no consensus as to what constitutes proper usage. To put it bluntly, the English language is a mess.

But English is a living language, and the very diversity that makes the English language messy also makes it vibrant.

8

You can "pop" a baby in Cambridge, England, but not in Cambridge, Massachusetts

*O*n October 30, 1997, in a Cambridge, Massachusetts, courtroom, British au pair Louise Woodward was found guilty of murdering eight-month-old Matthew Eappen. The child died on February 9, five days after Woodward called 911 to report that the baby was unconscious. The prosecution's case was based on autopsy reports that showed Matthew's injuries were caused by a violent shaking and having his head smashed against a hard surface.

British commentators were outraged by the verdict, and suggested that Woodward's quintessential British reserve throughout the trial might have been perceived by the American jury as the cold-heartedness of someone who could kill a baby. On November 10, however, Judge Hiller Zobel freed Louise Woodward. He reduced the charge to involuntary manslaughter, ruling that premeditation had not been proved.

In addition to her British diffidence, it might have been her "Britspeak" that predisposed an American jury against her. To paraphrase George Bernard Shaw, British English and North American English are two languages separated by an ocean. During the trial, Louise Woodward talked of "popping [quickly putting] the baby into bed." "Popping a baby," in America, carries connotations of abuse.

The war between the British and Americans may have ended in 1776, but the linguistic embers have been smoldering ever since. In the eighteenth and nineteenth centuries, American usage was constantly ridiculed in England. All the following words were assailed as vulgarisms: *to advocate, influential, lengthy, to locate, to oppose, to progress, reliable,* and *talented.* British writer Samuel Taylor Coleridge went so far as to denounce the word *talented* as "that vile and barbarous vocable."

Many of the critics of the dreaded "Americanisms" were Americans themselves, including the coiner of the term "Americanism," Princeton University president John Witherspoon. He wrote a series of articles in 1781 in which he denounced "corruptions," such as using *notify* instead of "inform," *mad* instead of "angry," and *clever* instead of "good." Needless to say, Witherspoon's efforts to stamp out these usages were futile, and today even the bible of proper English, *The Oxford English Dictionary,* acknowledges the use of all these words.

Time has not bridged the gulf between the two branches of the language. For example, let us return to "baby talk." In England, a nanny changes a baby's *nappy* and not its *diaper,* and pushes it in a *pram,* not a *baby carriage.* The baby's *crib* in the United States is referred to as a *cot* in England.

Differences in expressions create innumerable opportunities for embarrassment. In England, *keeping your pecker up* means having courage in the face of adversity. I remember reading how a Brit delivering a eulogy at an American funeral created consternation by advising the bereaved husband to "keep his pecker up." And speaking of expressions that end with the preposition "up," in England *washing up* is something you do to dishes after a meal, while in America the activity is performed on one's hands. In England, *knocking up* might be the action of somebody awakening another by knocking, or having a warm-up session in tennis, or preparing hastily, but it is not an act of impregnation.

Garments are a definite trouble zone. Picture the scene: you are an American invited for tea in Kensington Gardens, and you comment on the stylish pants of your hostess. This is bound to raise the odd eyebrow because in England, *pants* refers strictly to underwear. Less embarrassing vestmental gaffes would be referring to loose-fitting trousers as *overalls*, a *jumper* as a sleeveless dress, or a *vest* as a garment worn over a shirt. For in England, an *overall* is a coat-like outer garment to protect clothes, a *jumper* is a sweater, and a *vest* is worn under a shirt.

Minefields abound. Buttocks-related words also are problematic. *Fanny*, in England, does not refer to one's derriere but to one's pudendum. In England, *bum* never refers to a homeless person, only to that homeless person's posterior. And if you venture into a store in England and ask for *rubbers*, you'll probably be offered erasers. If it's condoms you need, ask for *sheaths*.

A Brit meeting his American CEO for the first time might announce that the company's software release in the UK went like a "bomb" and mention in passing, "Your wife is rather homely." If he wasn't terminated instantaneously, he could try to explain to his apoplectic boss that *bomb* in England means "great success" and *homely* means "pleasant."

In 1789, lexicographer Noah Webster predicted that, over time, British English and North American English would diverge to a point that they would become as different as "Dutch, Danish and Swedish are from German or from each other." Clearly, this has not come to pass.

On the contrary, having two dominant models of English has

created little confusion and has served to enrich the language. In a world with diminishing diversity, of greater concern is the possibility that the two major streams of English may one day flow indistinguishably. *Vive la différence!* Long may the Englishes be distinct.

9

African rhythms resonate in Black English

*I*n the 1830s, a cartoonist in Philadelphia published a series of popular cartoons that mocked the pretensions of the evolving Black middle class trying to "act White." One cartoon displayed a bewigged Black partygoer asking the following captioned question: "Shall I hab de honor to dance de next quadrille with you, Miss Minta?" Although despicably racist, these cartoons highlight the distinctive nature of Black English.

The language used by Blacks may have been distinct, but it was regarded as second rate. Even in the twentieth century, linguist George Philip Krapp characterized Black English as an inadequate imitation of British and American English that had lost all its links with its African heritage. In his 1925 book *The English Language in America*, he wrote: ". . . [I]t is probable that negro speech acquired its present pronunciation with 'r' omitted finally and before consonants through imitation of the imperfect imitation by ignorant negroes of the speech of cultivated white speakers. The negro omitted their r's because they heard no r's in the speech of their white superiors." Almost as disdainful is the characterization by H. L. Mencken in his opus *The American Language*: "The Negro dialect, as we know it today, seems to have been formulated by the song-writers for the minstrel shows; it did not appear in literature until the time of the Civil War . . . it was a vague and artificial lingo which had little relation to the actual speech of Southern blacks." Some recent pronouncements have been equally scurrilous. Contemptuous columnist and grammarian John Simon has ordained that "the constructions of Black English are the product not of a language with roots in tradition but of ignorance of how language works."

In spite of this condescension, however, it is now recognized by linguists that what used to be designated Black English Vernacular, and in recent years has been dubbed Ebonics, is not inferior but merely another of the multitudinous varieties of English spoken on the planet. In fact, Ebonics contains some useful refinements not available in Standard English. In a 1997 article in the magazine *Discover*, linguist John B. Rickford outlined some of the versatility of Ebonics, using as an example the verb "to run."

1) *He runnin.* ("He is running.")
2) *He be runnin.* ("He is usually running.")
3) *He be steady runnin.* ("He is usually running in an intensive, sustained manner.")
4) *He bin runnin.* ("He has been running.")
5) *He BIN runnin.* ("He has been running for a long time and still is.")

Rickford counters the claim that Ebonics is "lazy English," which arose because of its tendency to leave out consonants at the ends of words, especially if they come after another consonant. He explains that there is a structured set of rules in place that would not allow, for example, the omission of the final consonant in "pants." Rickford states that one can't delete "the second consonant at the end of a word unless both consonants are either voiceless, as with 'st' or voiced, as with 'nd.' In the case of 'pant' the final 't' is voiceless, but the preceding 'n' is voiced, so the consonants are both spoken."

Today, scholars generally agree that Ebonics gives voice to some African linguistic tendencies, and that these were not totally eradicated as the language evolved. Robert McCrum and Robert MacNeil, in *The Story of English*, relate that "[t]he African element in the English spoken by slaves on the plantation — known as Plantation Creole — was sustained for some time, since some African languages, Wolof in particular, were spoken in the southern states during the eighteenth century." On each plantation, there would be some slaves who would be esteemed by their peers for their knowledge of African languages.

An African heritage resonates through the speech patterns of Ebonics. For example, many West African languages don't possess the problematic English "th" sound. The lack of this consonantal combo may thus lead to *them* being rendered as *dem*. For similar reasons, Standard English consonant groupings like "st" or "sk" are likely to be rendered as just an "s" in Ebonics, so that *desk* becomes *des*. The linguist J. L. Dillard points out that African roots have in fact proliferated in other versions of American English. "There are details of pronunciation . . . in Southern White English which . . . even match Africanisms. Take the so-called plosive consonant — the pronunciation of 'beel' rather than 'bill' — which is characteristic of Ebonics. This plosive consonant exists in African languages. It's not characteristic in Northern White English. . . ." To account for this, it is useful to remember that, until the age of six, White and Black children grew up together on plantations, and the White children were often the minority group. Furthermore, all the nursing was entrusted to Black women.

Another African legacy in Ebonics, according to Geneva Smitherman, writing in *Black Talk*, is the power of the spoken word. According to Smitherman, "the African concept of 'Nommo,' the Word, is believed to be the force of life itself. To speak is to make something come into being; thus senior Black Americans will often use the cautionary statement 'Don't speak on it' in the face of some negative possibility." Smitherman has stated that from "[t]he sixties to the eighties, we were trying to get recognition for the language, that it had rules, it has a system, it has a pattern. Now we are at the point where we need a multilingual policy."

It was once felt that as more Blacks entered the mainstream the dialect would greatly fade. According to linguists, however, the current generation of inner-city youth employs the Black vernacular more than ever. The persistence of the dialect reflects an attitude that prizes cultural distinction. Ebonics endures because it fulfils a cultural need by enhancing Black solidarity. On the other hand, the inability of a Black person to speak Standard English can seriously impede his or her social and economic prospects.

Schoolteachers used to devote themselves to correcting Ebonics usage under the impression that they were thus imparting proper grammar to the Black student. *The Oxford Companion to the English Language* states that "because Black English is devalued . . . many teachers with excellent intentions continue to denigrate it in favor of standard English. Few such educators . . . have learned about the history and nature of Afro-American English, and fail to appreciate its diversity and logical integrity as a long-established variety of the language."

My view is that we should not teach Ebonics as a distinct language, but rather use it as a tool to improve an Ebonics-user's mastery of Standard English. As of yet, however, there appears to be no consensus as to the best way to teach Standard English to students who speak the Black dialect, and teachers are left to their own devices to find the most effective method.

10

Go know? Yiddishisms are popular!

*W*hile other languages treasure chastity, the English language tends to sleep with whoever it finds most attractive. In the twentieth century, one of its most common bedmates has been Yiddish. Countless Yiddishisms, such as *bagel* and *kibitz*, now pepper the mainstream vernacular.

Still, as a Jewish person, I am sometimes surprised to discover just how extensive these Yiddish inroads have become. Recently, I phoned an editor, who is not Jewish, to see if he had received the controversial book I wanted to review. He told me he had and that in his opinion it looked like "a bunch of *dreck*." This surprised me, but not because I held a contrary view of the book. No, what surprised me was the editor's knowledge of the word *dreck*, a Yiddish expression that means "crap" or "worthless thing."

Dreck is originally a word of German derivation, and it referred to excrement. According to Leo Rosten in *The Joys of*

Yiddish, in English, the word *dreck* has a particular application to the arts, so the editor's use of the word to describe a book was bang-on. I was surprised to learn that *dreck* had found its way into English dictionaries as far back as 1922, following its appearance in James Joyce's *Ulysses*: "Farewell. Fare thee well. Dreck!"

A Yiddish word that found its way into our language well before *dreck* is the word *chutzpah*. In Yiddish, *chutzpah* has only a negative meaning, that of "brazen effrontery or impudence." In English, however, *chutzpah* is a more expressive word. It is usually defined as "outrageous nerve," but this definition is invariably coupled with an explanation. Two favorite *chutzpah* examples are:

- someone who kills both parents and pleads mercy before the judge because he is an orphan;
- someone who reports her landlord for building-code violations when she's six months behind in the rent.

The Oxford English Dictionary's (OED) first citation for the word derives from London-born Israel Zangwill's *Children of the Ghetto* (1892) and it conveys a positive sense: "The national Chutzbah [*sic*], which is variously translated enterprise, audacity, brazen impudence and cheek." Seventy-four years later, *chutzpah* found a Canadian home when *Maclean's* magazine reported that Dr. Morton Shulman's most outstanding quality was *chutzpah* — "a combination of enormous self-confidence and indifference to what other people think."

When the word *chutzpah* is used in a political sense, the meaning is usually not complimentary and it describes "extreme gall." James Reston of *The New York Times*, assessing the sexual antics of presidential candidate Senator Gary Hart in 1987, said, "Mr. Hart's *chutzpa* has hit a new level of political arrogance." (One wonders at what level he would place President Clinton's *chutzpah* quotient.)

The 1950s and '60s saw an infusion of many Yiddish words

into the English language. Observe *nosh* ("light snack," 1955), *bobkes* ("nothing," 1958), *klutz* ("clumsy person," 1960), *kvetsh*, ("complain," 1964), and *shtik* ("show-business routine," 1965).

Since the 1960s, there has been a marked slowdown in the Yiddish linguistic invasion. The television program "Saturday Night Live," however, popularized two unlikely Yiddish candidates in the 1990s. In a segment entitled "Coffee Talk," Mike Myers played the character Linda Richman, who was prone to using the words *shpilkes* ("nervous energy") and *farklempt* ("bummed out" and "all choked up").

I suspect that certain Yiddish words get absorbed into English not because they introduce a new concept but because they're fun to say. After all, English has many colorful words to denigrate a person's character, but *shlemiel*, *shmo*, *shmuck*, *nudnik*, and *meshugenner* roll off the tongue with glee.

While it is easy to spot many Yiddishisms by their initial "sh" sound, in some cases the Yiddish pedigree isn't so obvious. The OED traces the word *mishmash* back to the Danish *misk-mask* and shows the word entering the English language in 1452. It was, however, early-twentieth-century New York Jews who popularized this vivid word, possibly because they found the double "sh" sound particularly appealing.

It is difficult to escape one's roots. I used the phrase *go know* several times to a non-Jewish business associate, who then informed me that he had never heard the expression. I checked in a phrase book which showed "*Go know* — Yinglish. From the Yiddish expression *Gey vays* (meaning, 'go know')." It said the expression could mean "How could I know?" or "How could you expect me to know?" or "How could anyone know?" So, inadvertently, I had been using a Yiddishism.

Go know?

11

It's an English world after all

*I*n his 1997 book, *English as a Global Language*, linguist David Crystal points out that "in 1950, any notion that English was a true world language was but a dim, shadowy, theoretical possibility, surrounded by the political uncertainties of the Cold War, and lacking any clear definition or sense of direction."

Of course, that was then. The spread of English in the latter half of this century has been nothing short of phenomenal. Now, fully one-fourth of the world's population is fluent in English. Presently, there are more first-language speakers of English than second-language speakers, but it is estimated that within ten years this situation will reverse because of population trends. Within fifty years there will be 50 percent more second-language speakers than first-language speakers.

A "New English" is evolving, wherever English is spoken as a second language around the world, and some of its phrases might be incomprehensible to the unilingual Standard English practitioner. For example, do you have any idea what this means? An Indian invites his *cousin-brother* to a *military hotel* on a *kutcha road* where people eat on *dining leafs*. Translation: He invites his "male cousin" to a "non-vegetarian restaurant" on a "dirt road" where the food is served on "banana leaves." Similarly, the Singaporean English word for food, *makan*, and the Nigerian English word for a roadside restaurant, *buka*, will not be understood by most non-local English-speakers.

This trend does not sit well with certain originators of the English language — namely, the English. Professor Randolph Quirk has said that when people refer to "Indian, Singaporean and Nigerian English and so forth, they are talking about a variation in which there is no native base to carry on the tradition. They are speaking a foreign language." In 1995, Prince Charles entered the fray complaining about the corrupting tendencies of non-British English and said the British version should lead the way as the world language.

With all due respect, esteemed professor and prince, if we didn't have these "corrupting" influences, English literature would be very impoverished. In any case, as Salman Rushdie has pointed out, "the English language ceased to be the sole possession of the English some time ago." Rushdie says that "those people who were once colonized by the language are now rapidly remaking it, domesticating it, becoming more and more relaxed about the way we use it. Assisted by the English language's enormous flexibility and size, they are carving out large territories for themselves within its front."

The Booker Prize is literature's version of the Academy Awards. Each year it is awarded to what is deemed to be the best English-language novel written by a resident of the United Kingdom, the Commonwealth, or South Africa. These are the birthplaces of some of the winners, since 1980: India (2), Australia (2), New Zealand (1), Nigeria (1), Japan (1), Egypt (1), South Africa (1), Ireland (1), Scotland (1), and Sri Lanka (1). The

1992 co-winner, Michael Ondaatje, was characterized in a 1993 *Time* magazine article as a "Sri Lankan of Indian, Dutch and English ancestry, educated in Britain, long resident in Canada, with siblings on four continents." The same article goes on to say that "five days earlier the Nobel Prize for Literature was awarded to Derek Walcott, a poet of African, Dutch and English descent, born in St. Lucia and commuting these days between Boston and Trinidad."

Writing in *Time* magazine, Pico Iyer has pointed out the extent to which the ethnic roots of these writers are integral to their literature. "[Kazuo] Ishiguro is a paradigm of the polycultural order, incarnating in his every sentence the effects of his mixed upbringing in England and Japan." Similarly, Booker Prize winner Keri Hulme, from New Zealand, incorporates Maori words and spirits in her novel, *The Bone People*.

In his preface to *English as a Global Language*, David Crystal suggests that while the world requires a common language of communication, there is also a "fundamental value to multi-lingualism, as an amazing world resource which presents us with different insights and perspectives, and thus enables us to reach a more profound understanding of the nature of the human mind and spirit."

Interestingly, in many places the English language is fulfilling both functions all by itself. Jamaican writer Mervyn Morris says, "One values greatly the creole because it expresses things about the Jamaican experience which are not available for expression in the same force in Standard English." Proficiency in Standard English, however, is important to Morris, "because we do not want to cut ourselves off from international communication."

For some, the devotion of some writers to the language of their former oppressors has been seen as a source of angst. According to Pico Iyer, writers such as Derek Walcott have used "English as a way to reclaim a heritage, and to take the instrument of imperialism and turn it upon itself."

In 1963, Indian writer Raja Rao commented: "English is not really an alien language to us. It is the language of our intellectual make-up — like Sanskrit and Persian was before — but not of our emotional make-up. We cannot write like the English. We should not. We can write only as Indians. We have grown to look at the large world as part of us. Our method of expression has to be a dialect which will some day prove to be as distinctive and colourful as the Irish or the American."

In any case, the price of having a world language is showing tolerance and an appreciation for its myriad flavors. Non-native speakers of English, who will soon outnumber native speakers, must have a sense of ownership in the global language.

12

So you think Canadian English isn't distinct, eh?

*W*riting in the 1960s, Walter Avis related the following anecdote in his introduction to *A Dictionary of Canadianisms on Historical Principles*. A Canadian shopping in a Chicago department store inquired as to where he might find *chesterfields* (Canadian English for "sofas") and was directed to the cigar counter. The culturally challenged chap soon discovered that in America *blinds* are "shades," *taps* are "faucets," *braces* are "suspenders," and *serviettes* are "napkins." I suspect, however, that if our shopping expedition were to take place today, his vocabulary would correspond to a much greater extent to American usage.

This is not to say that what is called Canadian English no longer possesses a distinctive vocabulary, just that some of the differences in vocabulary are narrowing. Considering the constant bombardment of Canada by American English, it is remarkable that Canadians have *any* remaining national speech characteristics. When two bordering nations, such as Canada and the United States, share a language, it is inevitable that the more frequently heard vocabulary will become the standard.

The apparent lack of distinct Canadian grammar or pronunciation makes Canadians seem indistinguishable from Americans to foreigners. Of course, as newspaper journalist Gerald Clark has pointed out, "the surest way of telling them apart is to make this observation to a Canadian." Seymour Lipset, in *Continental Divide*, states that "to justify separate national existence Canadians have deprecated American values and institutions. . . . Canadians have tended to define themselves not in terms of their own national history and traditions but by reference to what they are not: Americans."

Humorist Stephen Leacock said, "In Canada we have enough to do keeping up with two spoken languages without having to invent slang, so we just go ahead and use English for literature, Scotch for sermons and American for conversation." Mark Orkin, author of *Canajun, Eh?*, believes "language in Canada lacks the verbal fantasy and sheer uninhibited gusto of American English. . . . We are largely devoid of the verbal elan which produced such inspired Americanisms as 'crook,' 'belly laugh,' 'burp,' and 'OK.'"

In comparing British, American, and Canadian writing, in 1972, Margaret Atwood noted the unifying themes at the heart of each national literature. The motif in England is seen as "the island" — after all, an Englishman's home is his castle. The dominant American symbol is "the Frontier," which "suggests a place that is new where the old order can be discarded." In Canada, the central symbol in both English- and French-Canadian literature is "Survival, *la Survivance*." The main idea, for Atwood, is "hanging on, staying alive. Canadians are forever taking the national pulse like doctors at a sickbed: the aim is not to see whether the patient will live well but simply whether he will live at all. . . . Our central idea is . . . an almost intolerable anxiety."

Atwood believes Americans love and virtually worship success, whereas Canadians are suspicious of it. Hugh MacLennan remarked that Canadian culture reflects the fact that the three founding nationalities were defeated peoples: the French and the Scots by the English, the English by the Americans. Robertson Davies has pointed out that although Canada is a prosperous nation, "the miseries of its earliest white inhabitants are bred in the bone, and cannot, even now, be rooted out of the flesh."

MacLennan believed that Canada exhibits female characteristics, such as "the good woman's hatred of quarrels." For literary critic Mary Jean Green, it is "because female voices have a special resonance for the culture as a whole that, in Canada, women writers have assumed such an important role in defining a reality that is not uniquely feminine but rather, profoundly Canadian."

Perhaps these national traits explain what might be described as a tendency among Canadians, especially as compared to Americans, toward hedging and understatement. Something that might be described as "awesome" in the United States is more likely to be designated "not bad" by a Canadian, or, when we are at our most hyperbolic, as "okay." Ask an American how he's doing and the answer is liable to be "great." The Canadian is likely to answer "surviving."

And who other than a Canadian could express so many thoughts with a two-lettered interjection? Mark Orkin translates: "I'm walking down the street, eh? (Like this, see?) I had a few beers en I was feeling priddy good, eh? (You know how it is.) When all of a sudden I saw this big guy, eh? (Ya see.) He musta weighed all of 220 pounds, eh? (Believe me.) I could see him a long ways off en he was a real big guy, eh? (I'm not fooling.) I'm minding my own business, eh? (You can bet I was.)"

Perhaps the ubiquitous Canadian usage of *eh* is a way of asking for reassuring feedback, as if to say, "Do you?" or "Don't you think so?" Don't you think it's the most civilized way to end a sentence, eh?

13

Canadian dictionaries stand on guard for my identity

*W*hat has been called Canadian English is essentially a hybrid of American and British English and thus lacks a distinctive grammar, spelling, or pronunciation. The distinctiveness of Canadian English rests squarely in our vocabulary usage — in our "Canadianisms." In 1967, the editors of *A Dictionary of Canadianisms on Historical Principles* defined "Canadianism" as "a word, expression, or meaning which is native to Canada or which is distinctively characteristic of Canadian usage though not necessarily exclusive to Canada." Certain usages have a strong Canadian flavor. For example, the usage of the word *bellwether* as an indicator, as in a "bellwether riding," is more prominent in Canada than elsewhere.

Take the following passage: The *beerslinger* posted a sign warning that "*suckhole hosers* with *Molson muscles, rubbies,* and *shit-disturbers* are not welcome." No sirree. Folks were drinking *Bloody Caesars* and *brown cows* at the *booze can.* Heck, even the *Gravol* was free.

None of the italicized entries is likely to be found in your home dictionary, as they are all true-north Canadianisms. They find a home, however, in *The Canadian Oxford Dictionary*, released in June 1998. A little translation is in order for the non-partying or non-Canadian reader. A *beerslinger* is an informal term for a bartender; a *hoser* means a lout; a *rubby* refers to a derelict alcoholic known to mix rubbing alcohol with what he is imbibing; *Molson muscle* is a term for a beer-belly; *brown cow* and *Bloody Caesar* are names for cocktails in Canada; and a *booze can* is a term for an illegal bar, usually in someone's home. We now join Australia, New Zealand, and South Africa in having our own indigenous Oxford dictionary. And you thought that Canadian English was no more than the word *eh*, eh?

Lexicographically speaking, Canada has been particularly blessed of late. In 1983, Gage Publishing brought out the *Gage Canadian Dictionary*, and they've recently released an updated version, enhanced by 13,000 new entries, many of them drawn from the burgeoning fields of science and technology. The *ITP Nelson Dictionary* is encyclopedic in nature and is essentially a Canadian adaptation of the *American Heritage High School Dictionary*.

Of course if you spend any amount of time with Americans, they'll be sure to point out to you some of your quaint Canadianisms. When an American is nauseated or headachy she won't reach for *Gravol* or *ASA* but for "Dramamine" or "aspirin." *Javex*, *Varsol*, and *garburator* may be Canadian household items, but an American will not know what these terms mean and will refer to them instead as "chlorine bleach," "mineral spirits," and "garbage disposal unit."

Words and phrases that Canadians use every day are not to be found in most dictionaries. I discovered this recently when I ran a manuscript through my computer's spell-check. Words such as *anglophone* and *francophone* do not exist as legitimate entries on the database. Canadians are prone to use expressions such as

March break (school holiday in March), *seat sale* (airline tickets at a reduced price), and *book off* (stay home from work, especially when sick) without realizing that non-Canadians don't necessarily know what we are talking about.

In some cases, the usage of Canadianisms is restricted to a particular region of Canada. Take the expression *two-and-a-half* to refer to an apartment with a combined living room/bedroom, kitchen, and bathroom. This is strictly a Quebec English usage. Then again, I don't think too many Quebeckers are familiar with the Newfoundland *bangbelly*. It is a pudding, cake, or pancake consisting of a dumpling-like mixture that is fried, baked, or stewed. Few people outside of British Columbia would be familiar with the words *chuck* ("large body of water"), *oolichan* (type of fish), *skookum* ("big and powerful"), or *squamish* ("squally storm"). These are all words derived from the Chinook jargon, the trading language that in the early years of British Columbia was more widely used than English. Nor are most dictionaries likely to have the following words common in the Maritimes: *bedlamer*, *whitecoat* ("young harp seals"), and *mussel mud* ("mud rich in shells, used as fertilizer").

I was recently amused at hearing a PBS TV commentator refer to America as the planet's first pluralistic society. This statement, however, is not borne out by lexicographical data. For example, the word *multiculturalism* is not to be found in American dictionaries. It is one of the words deemed in *Trash Cash, Fizzbos, and Flatliners*, a 1993 book about neologisms, to be on the cusp of acceptance by dictionaries. It has, however, been a mainstream word in Canada since the 1960s.

It would appear that the route to a multicultural society in Canada is via our gullets. The dumpling-like Slavic *perogi*, the Greek dishes *tzatziki* and *souvlaki,* and the Arab eggplant dish *baba ghanouj* do not flavor American dictionaries such as *Webster's Third* or the *American Heritage*. All these dishes are to be found, however, in the *Gage, ITP Nelson,* and *Oxford*

Canadian dictionaries. Dining in Canada can be a distinct experience. You will not find any of these words in non-Canadian dictionaries: *poutine* ("french fries topped with cheese curds"), *tourtiere* ("French-Canadian meat pie"), *all-dressed pizza* (with all the trimmings), or *smoked meat* (cured beef similar to pastrami but more heavily smoked). *The Canadian Oxford Dictionary* even had the gastronomical sense to have an entry for *Montreal bagel*, which is defined as "a type of bagel, originally made in Montreal, which is lighter, thinner, and sweeter than other kinds of bagels."

The preface to *The Canadian Oxford Dictionary* states that it is the fruit of "five years of work by five Canadian lexicographers examining almost twenty million words of Canadian text held in databases representing over 8,000 different Canadian publications. Fiction and non-fiction books, newspapers, magazines, even theatre programs, grocery store flyers and Canadian Tire catalogues." Both the *ITP Nelson* and the *Gage Canadian* dictionaries are aimed at the school markets, and they are prescriptive in the sense that expletives are not included in either. Such is not the case with *The Canadian Oxford Dictionary*. Aside from *shit-disturber*, these are some of the other headwords that adorn page 1336: *shit-faced, shit for brains, shithead, shitless,* and *shitload*. Incidentally, in the United States a *shit-disturber* is more likely to be referred to as a "shit-stirrer."

Many common words acquire a Canadian flavor in *The Canadian Oxford Dictionary*. Take the word *shovel*. In the *Oxford English Dictionary*, a shovel is said to remove "quantities of earth, grain, coal or other loose material." In Canada, when we think of shoveling, the definitive object we think about is snow, and a *shovel* is defined as a "spadelike tool for shifting quantities of snow, coal, earth, etc." The verb *shovel* is described as "to clear (an area) of snow etc. using a shovel (shovelled the driveway)."

Even some of the most innocuous words can attain a Canadian

flavor. Definition (5) of the word *across* in *The Canadian Oxford* reads as follows: "Cdn (PEI) in or to Nova Scotia or New Brunswick (go across, come from across)." Similarly, one of the definitions of *away* is "Cdn (Nfld and Maritimes) in a place other than the speaker's home province or Atlantic Canada in general (they're from away)."

And of course, *The Canadian Oxford Dictionary* also features the countless hockey terms — such as *drop the gloves* and *dump and chase* — that pepper our lexicon. One could be excused at times for confusing Canadian politics with a hockey match. Take the following headlines that have graced Canadian newspapers in the 1990s: "Joe Clark must now stickhandle route to new federalism"; "Mr. Klein's entire government is based on the spin-a-rama"; "Joe Ghiz hangs up his skates because he is feeling too old and tired for the game of politics."

By the way, all three dictionaries feature ROTW ("rest of the world") words you'd find in other dictionaries.

14

Montreal English is a distinct lingo in a distinct society

You say tomayto
And I say tomahto
You say potayto
And I say potahto
— *"Let's Call the Whole Thing Off!"*

*A*s songwriter Ira Gershwin suggests, there are different ways to pronounce the names of foods — among other things. My daughter Jennifer, in her freshman year at Yale, discovered that her manner of pronouncing words such as *pasta* and *avocado* did not conform to the style defined by her largely American schoolmates. For when a Canadian says *pasta*, the "a" in the first syllable is pronounced like the "a" in "fat"; when an American says *pasta*, this vowel is pronounced like the "a" in "father." Jennifer has been advised to render her *avocado* as "avo-cah-do." She has also learned to eschew Canadianisms, such as asking someone if they got a *good mark* instead of the more proper "good grade."

My daughter's English might be distinctive not only by virtue of her Canadian citizenship. It might well be colored by living in Quebec, as well. We Quebec-Anglo mutants incorporate galli-cisms, such as *dépanneur* ("convenience store") and *metro* ("subway"), into our vocabulary. Sometimes the influence of French is insidious. In speaking English, we will occasionally employ words in a French context. We might use *conference* to mean "lecture" and *verify* to mean "inspect." Such usages are unique to speakers of Quebec English.

Our distinctive pronunciation even transcends country and province by having a metropolitan flavor. It's been said that when a Montrealer pronounces the first syllable of his city's name, it rhymes with "sun," whereas to most non-Montrealers, it rhymes with "gone."

Professor Charles Boberg of Montreal's McGill University is conducting a survey entitled "Dialect Topography of Montreal," in conjunction with Jack Chambers of the University of Toronto. They are "trying to discover what words are used by people of Montreal, and how they pronounce them." This is the first systematic analysis since 1958 of the way in which Montrealers speak English.

Here is a brief sampling of questions:

- What do you call the upholstered piece of furniture that three or four people sit on in the living room?
- For you, does VASE rhyme with "face," "days," "cause" or "has"?
- Do WHINE and WINE sound exactly the same? In other words, are the WH of whine and W of wine pronounced the same or different?
- Does the sch of SCHEDULE sound like "sch" in school, or "sh" in shed?

Montreal readers under the age of twenty-five might be surprised to learn that the definitive answer to the first question among octogenarians is "*chesterfield.*" This Canadianism became popular in the 1920s, but by the '70s its usage had started to wane.

Boberg said that when I phoned him and enunciated the word

Gazette, he surmised from the way I aspirated the final "t" that I was likely a Montrealer of Jewish descent. He added that, among Montreal Jews, words such as *my*, *five*, and *tie* have a "darker sound than in non-Jewish speech, so that 'line' can sound a little bit like 'loin,' 'tie' like 'toy.'" So not only was my speech distinctive because I was a Canadian, a Quebecker, and a Montrealer, it was even spiced by my being Jewish. Go know?

According to Boberg, "in western Canadian cities and perhaps even in Toronto, it is very difficult, if not impossible, to hear any differences in the way native-English-speaking members of different ethnic groups speak English, but in Montreal those differences can be quite pronounced, as between Anglos, Jews, and Italians, for instance."

Aside from French or ethnic influences, there is some particularity in how all Montrealers speak English. Professor Boberg says there are expressions such as "corner Peel" (a central Montreal street) that are uttered only by Montrealers. According to Boberg, Montrealers hear a distinction between the words *merry* and *marry* that is not widely discerned. "In most of Canada and in much of the US, these are the same (they both sound like 'merry'): in Montreal, many people make a distinction between them, with the a-sound of 'map' in 'marry' and the e-sound of 'met' in 'merry.'"

How we pronounce words is a matter that has more than mere academic relevance. Speech-recognition software is being developed, offering the possibility of manipulating a computer without a keyboard or a mouse. We'll have the freedom to ask our computer for a recipe while we're hanging our wallpaper. But speech recognition has been hampered by the multivaried dialects that people use. Dialect research of the type performed by Boberg is essential to bring this technology into real-world use, everywhere.

Part Three

Genealogy: The Pedigree of a Mongrel Language

English has by far the largest vocabulary of any language. Author Robert Claiborne has described words as "a kind of national resource; it is impossible to have too many of them." Occasionally, a word will appear *ex nihilo*, such as the word *googol* to describe a number as large as 1 followed by a hundred zeros (it was coined by mathematician Edward Kasner's nine-year-old nephew). This type of word formation is quite rare. Most words have fascinating histories, and in this segment we are going to examine some of the surprises secreted away in the origins of words.

15

The most famous word in the English language

*a*uthors Judith S. Neaman and Carole G. Silver, in *Kind Words*, state that "since the names of gods were considered identical with them, to speak a name was to evoke the divinity whose power then had to be confronted." In this spirit, the name Yahweh is so highly tabooed that devout Jews refer to God by the term *Adonai*, "Lord." As further prophylaxis, this euphemism itself should be mumbled.

Seen in this light, the long-standing proscription against the "f-word" might be seen as a profane equivalent to the divine injunction. Increasingly, however, one hears the word now being used in songs, movies, and books. Probably the last bastion of propriety in our libertine society is the newspaper. Michael Cooke, editor of the Vancouver *Province*, set the standard for use of the "f-word" in Canadian dailies: "Only if the prime minister said it in question period. And then only once." Seeing that I am not quoting any prime ministers, and so as to not to offend the capricious forces of the universe, I am euphemizing our "unmentionable" as the "f-word," "f___," "effed" when a past participle, and "effer" when a proper noun.

I am not alone in setting this word at the summit of our language's profanities. Edward Sagarin, in *The Anatomy of Dirty Words*, proclaims: "In the entire language of proscribed words . . . from the mildly unclean to the utterly obscene . . . one word reigns supreme, unchallenged in its preeminence. It sits upon a throne, an absolute monarch, unafraid of any princely offspring still unborn, and by its subjects it is feared, revered and loved, known by all and recognized by none." Hugh Rawson, in *Dictionary of Euphemisms*, adds his homage: "it hardly takes a genius to figure out this is the most distinguished of the four letter words."

Whence came our Sovereign?

It probably was originally a Germanic word related to the Middle Dutch *fokken*, "to thrust" or "copulate with," the Norwegian *fukka*, "copulate," and the Swedish *fukka* and *fock*, meaning "copulate" and "penis" respectively. There is no truth to the many acronyms dreamed up in folk etymology to explain it, such as "Fornication Under the Consent of the King" or "For Unnatural Carnal Knowledge."

Its first appearance in written form comes in the year 1503. There is, however, a verbal reference to "John le Effer" in 1278, for even in pre-Chaucerian times its written form might have been taboo. By Shakespeare's era it was considered vulgar, and it seems the Bard disguised the "f-word" in *Henry IV Part 2* when the character Pistol says, "A foutra for the world and worldlings base." It also masquerades as "firk" and "fut" elsewhere in Shakespearean plays.

It is one of the five words employed as a synonym for the Italian verb *fottere* in an Italian-English dictionary of 1598. The other four synonyms are *jape*, *occupy*, *sard*, and *swive*. The only one of these four that survives is *occupy*, and it was purged of its sexual sense and returned to lexicographic respectability by the early nineteenth century.

Canadian playwright John Gray explains the strength of the "f-word" as a form of punctuation: "It rolls off the lips like a spit, an exclamation point." Roy Blount, in the introduction to his book *The F-Word*, describes the sound of the word as "like a suction-cup arrow hitting a wall. Or someone pulling it off. . . . It's a fun word to say."

In recent years, our outcast word has been allowed out of the closet and can be found in some dictionaries. But this is a rather recent development. It was first openly printed in the United States only in 1926. It appeared in James Joyce's *Ulysses* in 1922, but it wasn't until after a court battle that this book was granted entry into America, in 1933. D. H. Lawrence's *Lady Chatterley's Lover*, which also makes extensive use of the word, was not given court clearance until 1959.

Even such salty characters as H. L. Mencken and Norman Mailer eschewed the use of the "f-word." Mencken, in his opus *The American Language*, leapfrogs from *fubar* ("effed" up beyond all recognition) to *fudge*. Even as late as 1944, he wrote an article in *American Speech* entitled "American Profanity" without once printing the word. Mailer, in his 1948 book *The Naked and the Dead*, avoided its usage in favor of *fug*. Because of this bowdlerization, the irrepressible Dorothy Parker chided him at a cocktail party: "So you're the young man who can't spell f___." In 1954, Dr. Leo Stone, in *The International Journal of Psycho-Analysis*, wrote an article on obscene language and consulted many dictionaries devoted to vulgar language but couldn't find a listing for the "f-word."

Alas, because of centuries of neglect, we cannot properly study the most famous word in the English language. Richard Dooling, in his investigation *Blue Streak*, laments, "The casual vulgarian may shrug his shoulders at the systematic, invidious discrimination that kept the f-word out of dictionaries for five

hundred years. . . . The record of the word's youth is lost forever!"

P.S. Alas, since I first wrote this, the "f-word" has been stealing its way into the formerly pristine pages of newsprint.
Therefore, my self-imposed injunction against using it in print is
henceforth terminated. Allow me to demonstrate the acrobatic
versatility of the "f-word" in the following passage culled from
Stephen Burgen's *Your Mother's Tongue*: "Fuck is the English
word par excellence, enlisted to serve as any and every part of
speech. Is there any other language where it is possible to construct a sentence such as, 'Fuck me. I'm fucked if I fucking know
what to fucking do. The fucking fucker fucking fucked up and
fucked off,' which while it is semantic rubbish, is capable of
being understood?"

16

The thought of food is food for thought

*O*ften, a new word will remind us of an old one. The homophones *muscle* and *mussel*, for example, both descend from the same root, the Latin *musculus*, literally, "little mouse." John Ayto, in *Dictionary of Word Origins*, tells us that in the fifteenth century *musculus* was "applied to the shellfish [*mussel*] because of a similarity in shape and color," and to *muscle* in the sixteenth century "because the shape and movement of certain muscles beneath the skin, such as biceps, reminded people of a mouse."

And if it is true that "we are what we eat," then, etymologically speaking, we are all cannibals. In *Ladyfingers & Nun's Tummies*, Martha Barnette explains what we are eating, from our heads to our toes.

The term *a head of cabbage* is redundant, it turns out, as cabbage descends from the Old French *caboce*, which literally means "head." Etymologically, that cabbage may be topped with *capelli d'angelo*, angel hair pasta, made of extremely thin noodles as fine as the hair of an angel. Moving on down the face, we have the round, convex pasta known in Italian as *orecchietta* ("little ears"), and we have "black-eyed peas," *linguine* ("little tongues"), and *saltimbocca*, an Italian dish of veal and ham supposedly so succulent that it means "leaps into the mouth."

Ms. Barnette informs us that the English language borrowed *pretzel* from German in the nineteenth century. Etymologically, a pretzel is a "little arm," and "these twisted biscuits were supposedly designed by European monks as symbols of arms obediently folded in prayer." Not surprisingly, *fingers* figure in the names of many foods. There is, of course, *ladyfingers*, long, oval-shaped sponge cakes. A less obvious finger food is the *date*. It comes from the Old French *date* and the Latin *dactylus*, which meant "finger." The term was originally applied because of the resemblance of a date to a little brown finger.

Moving down the body to our more private domains, we have the hunks of cheese from Galicia known as *tetilla* because of their distinctive round shape. Turks must also see a resemblance to a woman's anatomy in the pastry *kadin gobegi*, because that name means "woman's belly button." The Aztecs applied their word for testicle, *ahuacatl*, to a fleshy fruit with a similar shape. The Spanish conquistadors took this word over as *aguacate* and soon it was transformed into *avocado*, the Spanish word for "advocate." There is also *salep*, a starchy preparation of the dried tubers of various orchids* used in cooking and formerly in medicine; its name comes from the Arabic *kusa-'l-ta'lab*, meaning "fox's testicles."

Rounding out the body, we offer the Turkish entree *kadin-budu koefte*, which translates as "women's thigh meatballs," and we have the German name for a clove of garlic, *knoblauchzehe*, "garlic toe." Beneath the toe can be found the flatfish *sole*, which, like the sole on the bottom of the foot, derives from the Latin *solea*, which originally meant "sandal."

---

* Interestingly, the Greek word for testicles is "orchis."

The etymological origins of some foods might convince fastidious eaters to finally become vegetarians. Take lobster. Its name is rooted in the Latin *locusta*, "locust," because of a supposed resemblance between the crustacean and a grasshopper. If you covet pasta such as *bozzoli* and *vermicelli*, etymologically, you are lusting for "cocoons" and "little worms."

When eating Italian food, be prepared to get everything in the kitchen, and possibly even the kitchen sink. In Jay Jacob's *The Eaten Word*, we learn that Italian cuisine might include radiators, sewer pipes, the beards of goats and monks, hunchbacks, nuns' thighs, St. Agatha's breasts, nipples of the Virgin, eyes of the mother-in-law, rifles, sheet music, and a thousand infantrymen.

Jacob tells us that, unlike French cuisine, Italian food has ascribed the origins of its dishes "not to the Beautiful People but to ordinary working stiffs," such as rabbis, woodcutters, hunters, shoemakers, sailors, and prostitutes. *Marinara* sauces were credited to sailors because their preferred meatless dishes were made with ingredients less apt to spoil at sea. Dishes prepared *alla boscauilo* ("woodcutter's style") or *alla cacciatore* ("hunter's style") contain mushrooms, which would be easy pickings for someone who frequents forests. *Polla alla scarpiello*, "chicken shoemaker's style," is supposedly thus named because it is so delicious that people's fingers fly to their lips as fast as a shoemaker puts tacks in his mouth. Etymologists are divided on how *spaghetti alla puttanesca* received its name. Some believe its source was busy Neapolitan prostitutes who were able to prepare it quickly in between tricks; others believe it refers to the seductive aroma that induced innocent pedestrians into carnal liaisons.

Italian food doesn't own a monopoly on notoriously named dishes. The Greek lamb dish *arni kleftico* owes its name to the habit of Greek bandits who, after stealing people's food, would cook it in paper packets to mask the pungent aroma. Literally, *arni kleftico* means "stolen lamb," *kleftico* being a Hellenic cousin to the English *kleptomaniac*.

The human mouth is the conduit for both incoming food and outgoing words. Notwithstanding my having just "worded your eats," take heart that you're only reading, as opposed to eating, my etymologically unsavory words. *Bon appetit!*

17

What's in a nym?

*A*dmit it. Above all, you covet immortality. And now I will reveal the secret of how to attain this everlasting state — for your name.

You can have a comet named after you, which is the method used by Alan Hale and Thomas Bopp, or a disease, which is the technique employed by Dr. Parkinson. Alternatively, your ideas might give birth to adjectives — it worked for Freud, Machiavelli, and Christ.

And then there is that understated, insidious, lower-case type of immortality. Just as we forget that words such as *radar* and *scuba* have acronymic roots, we forget that words such as *shrapnel* and *silhouette* once came from actual people.

The Greeks had a word for people who live on in everyday conversations — *eponumos*, "named one," from which English takes the word *eponym*. Eponyms come in several forms. There are compound and attributive constructions — such as *loganberry*, named after nineteenth-century American lawyer James H. Logan, and *leotard*, named after the nineteenth-century trapeze artist Jules Léotard, who fashioned the tight-fitting garment.

Eponyms can also be derivative words — such as *bowdlerize*, "to expurgate prudishly," named after one Thomas Bowdler, whose mission in life was to render the Bard decent enough for a gentleman to read aloud in the company of a lady, and *gardenia*, named after Alexander Garden.

An eponym can also be a blended word. Eighteenth-century American politician Elbridge Gerry's redrawing of the map of the voting districts of Massachusetts was said to resemble a salamander. "Gerry" was wed to the last syllable of "salamander" to produce *gerrymander*, which is defined as "to divide a state, county, or city into voting districts to give unfair advantage to one party in elections."

Some eponyms are merely the surnames of individuals transferred into words. Examples of such are *boycott*, *bloomer*, *cardigan*, *doily*, and *sandwich*.

There are many colorful stories surrounding eponyms. Legend has it that John Montagu, the Earl of Sandwich, once spent twenty-four hours at a gaming table with no sustenance other than some cold meat placed between slices of toast by his manservant. This crude culinary technique apparently predated Montagu, but remained nameless until our gaming Earl gave his title to it.

It would appear that history has *lynched* the wrong Lynch. Most dictionaries have pinned the origins of this extrajudicial means of execution on eighteenth-century American Colonel Charles Lynch. A consensus has since arisen that it was his contemporary, Colonel William Lynch, who organized extralegal trials in Virginia, who is the father of this eponym.

The word *silhouette* comes from the eighteenth-century French minister of finance Etienne de Silhouette. Silhouette's attempts at budget restraint were unpopular, and originally the phrase *à la silhouette* meant "cheap." How his name became associated with the partial shadow portraits we call silhouettes is a matter of conjecture. Some say the incomplete portraits are associated with his cheapness, or the brevity of his term. Others say that Silhouette enjoyed making these portraits himself.

Silhouette's compatriot, Joseph Ignace Guillotin, is not, as would seem logical, the inventor of the guillotine. It was his idea, however, that all Frenchmen, and not only noblemen, have access to this "humanitarian" form of execution. As Guillotin put it: "the mechanism falls like thunder. The head flies off; blood spurts; the man is no more."

A word of warning is in order if you want to become an eponym. You might have to wait until you're dead to join the ranks. If you're the patient sort and are not fazed by this precondition to membership, here are a few suggestions. Probably, the best field to go into is science. Scores of scientists have words named after them. Observe *ampere* (named after André Marie Ampère), *curie* (Marie and Pierre Curie), *fermion* (Enrico Fermi), *galvanize* (Luigi Galvani), *ohm* (Georg Simon Ohm), *pasteurize* (Louis Pasteur), *volta* (Alessandro Volta), and *watt* (James Watt).

An alternate route is to become associated with a shrub, or be French — or both. Observe *begonia* (named after Michel Bégon), *magnolia* (Pierre Magnol), *fuchsia* (Leonhard Fuchs), *poinsettia* (Joel Robert Poinsett), *camellia* (Georg Josef Kamel), *chauvinism* (Nicolas Chauvin), *sadism* (the Marquis de Sade), *pompadour* (the Marquise de Pompadour), *leotard* (Jules Léotard), and *nicotine* (Jean Nicot).

If you seek an immortal name, do not become a famous painter or musician. These fields are rather under-represented in eponyms. Great names such as Mozart, Beethoven, and Rembrandt have not achieved the eponymous status that they merit.

Eponyms welcome the most recent member to the *nym* clan. Other family members — including acronym, antonym, heteronym, homonym, metonym, pseudonym, and synonym — are pleased to add *retronym* to their ranks.

Frank Mankiewicz, a onetime aide to American Senator Robert Kennedy, coined the word *retronym* to describe the union of adjectives to previous solitary nouns. *Retronym* is itself a marriage between the Latin *retro* (backward) and the Greek *onym* (name). *The Oxford Companion to the English Language* characterizes a retronym as a "phrase coined because an expression once used alone needs contrastive qualification; acoustic guitar because of electric guitar . . . mono sound equipment because of stereo sound equipment."

In bygone days, one could designate things using only nouns. A book was a book and coffee was coffee. Now we must specify whether we're talking about a hardcover or softcover book (not to mention electronic or non-electronic) and specify one of the myriad coffee varieties available to us. Technological innovations of the eighteenth and nineteenth centuries spawned a plethora of new vocabulary. "Telephone" came into the language in 1849, "typewriter" in 1868, "television" in 1907, and "movie" in 1912. Due to technological advances, the above singular inventions have turned into the following retronyms: *rotary phone, manual typewriter, black-and-white television,* and *silent movie.*

(For younger readers, perhaps I should explain the anachronistic *typewriter.* It is a single font, mechanical system for applying ink to paper that handled only alphanumeric characters. Originally, the word referred to the person who operated the machine — later *typist* — not the machine itself.)

Remember when people just received mail? Now it might be *certified mail, priority mail, e-mail, voice mail, snail mail, fax mail, ZapMail* — not to mention *blackmail* and *greenmail.* Once upon a time, baseball was just baseball and a pitcher was just a pitcher. *Night baseball* and *relief pitchers* robbed us of this simplicity. And now, strangely, one must specify if a volunteer is a *paid volunteer* or a *volunteer volunteer.*

Any change in society might necessitate a retronym. The appearance on the scene of the "self-serve" filling station gave rise to the term *full-service* station, where, incidentally, you can buy unleaded or retronymic *leaded gasoline*. Likewise, the performance of circumcisions for medical reasons created the retronym *ritual circumcision*. The greater reliance on drugs to mediate behavior necessitates the term *talk therapy*. With the development of the synthetic oil Olestra, we now have a *fat-free fat*. So what was previously just called fat is now, retronymically speaking, *fat-fat*.

In the old days, if you made a grocery list it might read: chips, milk, peanut butter, coffee, beer, and gum. Now we must specify if the chips are potato, corn, or tortilla; if the milk is skim milk or whole milk; whether the peanut butter is chunky or smooth; whether the coffee is regular, instant, or decaf; whether the beer is light or full; whether the gum is sugarless or not.

Marketing creates its own retronyms, because even "regular" Coke could be Real Coke, Coke Classic, or Caffeine-free. William Safire remarked that the makers of artificial eggs refer to their "rival product (shot through with cholesterol and nourishment) not as mere eggs, but as shell eggs." He also noticed the retronymic term *frozen concentrate*, necessitated by the creation of *unfrozen concentrate*. In all these examples, a true retronym, before the social or technological change that spawned it, would seem pointlessly redundant.

Retronyms need not have a technological base. *Jewish ghetto* is a case in point. The original "ghetto" was a Jewish quarter in Venice in 1516, which had previously been the site of a cannon foundry. *Getto* is the Italian word for "foundry." Later, the word *ghetto* came to mean the Jewish quarter of any city. Near the end of the nineteenth century, the sense was extended to refer to any poor neighborhood populated by a minority racial or cultural group.

Similarly, once *Italian Mafia* was a wholly redundant term. Increasingly, however, the term *mafia* is used to apply to ethnic backgrounds other than Italian.

What retronyms beckon in our ever-changing world? Judging by Deep Blue's victory over Garri Kasparov, *human chess champion* is a safe bet. *Silent computers* and *phoneless cars* loom on the horizon. In view of the ever-increasing fears about sexually transmitted diseases, *modemless sex* is another retronymic possibility. With the computer variety of sex you might still contract a virus, but at least it will be your hard disk and not you that will be crashing.

18

My southern neighbors, the Freeds?

*J*ust as Canada and Canadians have been evolving over time, so have the meanings of *Canada* and *Canadian*. The word *Canada* is derived from the Iroquoian *kanata*, meaning village. *Canadian* referred first to the native population, then strictly to French settlers, before it became the designation for all the people of the new land. The first usage in *The Oxford English Dictionary* dates to 1568: "How these Canadians doe chase the dere and other wilde beastes."

There were many other names suggested for the new land. Among those suggested were Tuponia, an acrostic for The United Provinces of North America, and the ugly-sounding Efisga, which was a combination of the first letters of England, France, Ireland, Scotland, Germany, and Aboriginal lands. But thankfully, the name Canada won out. There is thus a certain logic to the name of our country, implying as it does a pioneering spirit forged from the land.

There is no similar tale to relate about the origin of the name chosen for both the western hemisphere's two interconnected continents and our neighbor to the south. I speak, of course, of America. To paraphrase Churchill, never in the course of history has so much been named for one person for so little reason.

America was named for one Amerigo Vespucci, the supposed intrepid discoverer of the New World. But Vespucci was undeserving of this accolade. Vespucci had made three or four trips to *Mundus Novus*, "the New World," but either as a passenger or a minor officer. By all accounts he was not a distinguished seaman. However, in 1504, a publication of anonymous letters entitled *Nuovo Mondo* circulated in Florence, which claimed that Vespucci had captained all the intercontinental voyages.

It so happened that a German, Martin Waldseemuller, a teacher at a small French college, was working on a revised edition of the works of Ptolemy in 1507. He decided to adorn it with maps of the world he called "Cosmographia." He came across the Florentine letters extolling Vespucci and decided to honor him by naming the New World after him. Since Vespucciland didn't have a musical lilt to it, he opted for Vespucci's Christian name. He didn't like the sound of Amerigo or Amerige as geographical entities, so he translated Amerigo into the Latin *Americus* and then into the feminine form *America*, on the grounds that Asia and Europe (Europa) were also feminine forms.

In a 1513 edition of his book, Waldseemuller jettisoned America and replaced it with the prosaic *Terra Incognita*. By then, however, the name America had grown shallow roots. It would take another forty years for people to refer to the New World as America, and even then it referred only to the South American continent.

An *American*, like a *Canadian*, in early usages, referred strictly to the aboriginal population. In fact, the British writer Joseph Addison used the term *American* as a synonym for

"Indian" well into the eighteenth century. Colonists were called "transplanted Englishmen."

During the Revolutionary War, many called the new country the United Colonies. Those who started the insurrection didn't think of themselves as Americans. They were British and darn proud of it. The term *American* was a descriptive rather than an emotional designation. When Thomas Jefferson wrote that he wanted to return to his "own country," he was referring to Virginia. It took quite a while for an *American* consciousness to develop. In 1765, Christopher Gadden of South Carolina bemoaned, "There ought to be no New England men, no New York etc., known on the continent, but all of us Americans."

In the early years of the nascent land, consideration was given to renaming the country. Many felt that "the United States of America" was unsatisfactory. Bill Bryson points out in *Made in America*: "For one thing, it didn't allow for a conventional adjectival form. One would have to be a United Statesian . . . or an American, thus arrogating to ourselves a title that belonged equally to the inhabitants of some three dozen other nations on two continents."

Several alternative names to America were suggested. Among them were Alleghania, Appalachia, Columbia, Usona, and Fre(e)donia. Thankfully, none of these monikers garnered much support. Who would want to have the Freeds or Fredes as their neighbors?

Yes, America is a pretty name. Coincidentally, one of Vespucci's customers at his shipping supply company in Seville, Spain, was a man said to have "discovered" the land named after Vespucci. I speak, of course, of Christopher Columbus. But Columbus is no more deserving of the honor history has accorded him than was Vespucci. El Salvador was the closest Columbus came to mainland United States of America, whereas the explorer John Cabot reached the Canadian Maritimes.

After the Revolutionary War, otherwise known as the War of Independence, the honoring of a British hero like Cabot was anathema to Americans, and Columbus was chosen instead for exaltation. This was, however, unnecessary. For the name John Cabot was in fact an anglicized form of the Italian Giovanni Caboto.

19

Paparazzi and Princess Diana — both born in 1961

*Q*uestion: What do the words *malapropism*, *quixotic*, and *paparazzi* have in common? Answer: They are among only a handful of words that are derived from fictional characters.

Malapropism comes from Mrs. Malaprop, a character in Richard Sheridan's play *The Rivals* who is prone to replacing words with similar-sounding ones; *quixotic* recalls the dreamy, impractical hero of Cervantes's epic *Don Quixote*; and *paparazzi* is borrowed from an invasive photographer surnamed Paparazzo in Federico Fellini's 1959 movie *La Dolce Vita*.

Occasionally, a word that has hardly ever been uttered is suddenly released from obscurity. With the death of Diana, the Princess of Wales, and the alleged involvement of press photographers in the accident, the word *paparazzi* leapt to everyone's lips. But let us look back on the evolution of the word.

In 1958, celebrities regularly congregated at Rome's legendary Via Veneto. A photographer named Tazio Secchiaroli discovered that editors, tired of having to rely on glossy studio handouts, would pay him handsomely for revealing shots of the stars, so he set up shop where the stars came out to play. Fellini was toying with the idea of making a movie about café society anyway, and when he saw some of the handiwork from Secchiaroli's candid camera, he based a character in *La Dolce Vita* on him and named him Paparazzo. The name was particularly appropriate since, in some Italian dialects, *paparazzo* is a term for a buzzing insect. Therefore, in the case of *paparazzi*, we have the pluralized form of an eponymous word named after an onomatopoeic fictional character that is based on a real person.

By 1961, the words *paparazzo* (singular) and *paparazzi* (plural) were born in Italian to describe a photographer who harasses celebrities. Ironically, 1961 also marks the birth year of Diana Spencer, later to be Princess of Wales.

Paparazzi migrated to the English language in 1968. *The Oxford English Dictionary*'s first citation quotes this 1968 excerpt from *The Daily Telegraph* (London): "The anticipated horde of detested paparazzi — those scavenging Italian street photographers whose sole purpose appears to be to make every film celebrity's life a misery."

By 1972, *paparazzi* had crossed the ocean and the word was surfacing in legal cases. That year *The New York Times* said that "United States District Court Judge Irving Ben Cooper ruled yesterday that the activities of Ronald E. Galella, the self-styled paparazzo photographer, had 'relentlessly invaded the right to privacy of Mrs. Aristotle Onassis.'"

Five years later, a Canadian was deemed *paparazzi*-worthy and was somewhat more tolerant of their intrusiveness. *Maclean's* magazine reported in 1977 that "[i]f Margaret [Trudeau] was troubled by the public or the paparazzi that followed her during her New York stay, she certainly didn't show it."

Many words with a specific meaning go through a process of generalization, enlarging the sense of the word. The word *barn* originally referred to a place for storing barley, being a blend of *bere* ("barley") and *aern* ("house"). It then developed the added sense of storing any grain, and later of storing anything. Similarly, *manufacture* originally meant to "make by hand" and then only later to "make in any manner." *The Barnhart Dictionary Companion* in 1983 demonstrated this tendency in the word *paparazzi*. The word is used to describe a photographer's search for every detail in any subject: "But even the beings that have become extinct usually have approximately living counterparts that Attenborough and his camera crews can pursue as they snoop like scientific paparazzi on the private lives of all creatures big and small."

One senses in the aftermath of the death of the Princess of Wales, and the anger being directed toward aggressive photographers, that not only is there a process of generalization occurring with the objects of the attention of paparazzi, but the word *paparazzi* is being extended to include a greater spectrum of photographers than previously. *Paparazzi* are defined by most dictionaries as freelance photographers who pursue celebrities to take their pictures. Whereas previously the activity of pursuit or stalking was the operative condition for one to be labeled *paparazzi*, the sense of the word can now extend to refer to any aggressive photographer.

Although the term *paparazzi* from its inception has always held a pejorative connotation, its sense seems to be deteriorating even more. References to paparazzi as "assassins" and "carrion of fame" may lead to an association of the word with the idea of a pernicious hunter.

What else can we expect of *paparazzi*? With the tendency of English words to become shorter — *pants* were originally *pantaloons*, *piano* was *pianoforte*, and *wig* was *periwig* — count on *paparazzi* one day becoming *pap*, or *razzi*.

20

The full monty – dressed and undressed

*W*hile surfing the Net recently, I came across this anecdote related by British writer Nigel Rees. An American businessman was addressing a group of English entrepreneurs. He wanted to make the point that to earn a profit it is necessary to invest. The folksy saying "You got to spend a dollar to earn a dollar" came to mind, but since dollars were foreign to his audience, he changed the currency unit and stated, "You got to spend a penny to earn a penny." To his chagrin, this comment sent his assemblage into paroxysms of laughter. Why? Because to an Englishman, the expression *spend a penny* means going to the bathroom.

Many expressions that were born in the United States have eventually found their way into the British lexicon. For example, the expression *the whole nine yards* was coined in the United States and became common in Britain in the 1950s. The reverse trend is not as common, and I suspect not too many North Americans would be aware that *spending a penny* has a lavatory sense. Occasionally, however, a British expression will migrate westward. Such is the case with the term *the full monty*, because of the phenomenal success of the 1997 movie of the same name. The expression has been around in England for over fifteen years and it has been used to convey the sense of "the whole thing."

For a relatively new expression, details about its origin are obscure. *The Oxford English Dictionary* quotes K. Howarth, writing in 1985 in *Sound Gradely*: "Full-monty, everything included; a thorough display — no messing about." Writer Michael Quinion says that the first reference to *the full monty* that he encountered was in the book *Street Talk, the Language of Coronation Street*, published in 1986. After that, he found a reference in a 1989 edition of *The Guardian*. "What we're after is a live skeleton — the full monty." According to William Safire, in 1993 *The Glasgow Herald* described a diner "tucking into the full monty — bacon, sausage, eggs, and black pudding." The only reference to the expression found in the Southam News network is from *Broadcast News*, a television listing, in the following 1995 quote by Paul McCartney: "Does the world need a three-quarter Beatles record? But what if John was on, the three of us and John, like a real new record. If only we could pull off the impossible. That would be more fun, a bigger challenge — just the full monty."

There is no shortage of theories, however, as to the expression's origin. Here's a sampling:

- It was invented in the early 1980s by British comedian Ben Elton, possibly modeled on the expression *the whole shebang*.
- It refers to bales of wool imported from Montevideo, Uruguay.
- It refers to a pompous Field Marshal Bernard Montgomery parading with all his medals, or his habit of eating a large breakfast, or his meticulous battle plans.
- It refers to being dressed "to the nines" for a wedding while

being outfitted by the haberdashery firm Montague Burton. According to Nigel Rees, its founder, Sir Montague Burton (1885–1952), would supply "a full suit and accessories to purchasers, especially those being demobilized from the forces."

- It refers to the breakfast a certain Mrs. Montague served at the Lennox Café in West Sussex.
- It's derived from a television commercial for fruit juice in which someone asks for "the full Del Monte."
- It is gamblers' jargon referring to the pot, or kitty, derived from an old card game named monte.
- It's derived from Australian slang in which a *monty* is a bet (especially on a horse) that's a sure thing.

For those who haven't yet seen the movie *The Full Monty*, let me give you a brief synopsis: six unemployed steelworkers from Sheffield, England, form a male strippers' group, and, unlike a teasing Chippendale act, they provide their audience with full frontal nudity — *the full monty*.

In North America, it is this denuding interpretation that is becoming the phrase's definitive sense. William Safire cites the following story from the San Diego *Union Tribune*: the Carlsbad City Council had enacted a "zoning restriction to avert garishness." The newspaper remarked, "Carlsbad has reached the point where it can afford to go the full monty — full frontal snobbery."

Writing in his column "Among the New Words" in *American Speech*, the journal of the American Dialect Society, Wayne Glowka cites the following "metaphoric reference to nudity" in the movie section of the Boston *Herald*: "Apparently Tinseltown is atwitter over *Boogie Nights*, the New Line Cinema flick where Mark Wahlberg, 26, does the Full Monty, snorts coke and God knows what else as porn star Dirk Diggler."

The expression makes its way into the recently published *Oxford Dictionary of New Words*, with the following 1995 citation from *The Guardian*: "When conducting a funeral he wears the full monty: frock coat, top hat and a Victorian cane with metal tip." Glowka also cites a funereal scene from a Masterpiece Theater production a few years ago of *The Politician's Wife*. In it, a character referring to the recently departed says, "Well, they gave him the full monty."

This just goes to prove that when performing the full monty, clothes can be donned as well as doffed. It's just unfortunate that, in the former instance, someone had to die.

21

One man's corruption is another man's commonality

*F*ebruary 1884 marks the commencement, arguably, of the greatest feat of scholarship in the history of mankind. *The New English Dictionary on Historical Principles*, containing all the non-obscene words in the English language between A and Antyteme, was published in Britain. Each word was followed by a definition and by supporting citations from a wide range of literature.

The goal of this lexicographical endeavor was to "present in alphabetical series the words that have formed the English vocabulary from the time of the earliest records (c. A.D. 740) down to the present day with all the relevant facts concerning their form, sense-history, pronunciation, and etymology." The man chosen to head this august enterprise was James Augustus Henry Murray, a Scottish-born schoolteacher, bank clerk, and self-taught philologist. He thought the process would take twelve years and envisaged six volumes covering 6,400 pages. Instead, like Moses, his meandering took forty years and consisted of 15,000 pages.

Murray was working on the letter U when he died in 1915 at the age of seventy-eight. His assistants finished the last segment, Wise to Wyzen, in 1928. For some reason, the XYZ segment had been completed earlier. In 1933, a slightly updated version was issued under the name it has had ever since, *The Oxford English Dictionary* (OED). Because new words and usages have come into the English language, several other supplements were added between the years 1957 and 1986. In 1989, the OED issued a second edition in twenty volumes. Because of the existence of the OED, more is known about the history of English than about that of any other language.

The first English dictionary was Robert Cawdrey's *Table Alphabeticall of Hard Words*, published in 1604 replete with 2,560 entries. It was designed for "Ladies, Gentlewomen, or any other unskillful persons" to help them understand and use foreign borrowings. The introduction to the second volume of the OED states that "if there is any truth to the old Greek maxim that a large book is a great evil, English dictionaries have been steadily growing worse since the inception nearly four centuries ago. . . . It is like placing the original acorn beside the oak that has grown out of it." The second edition of the OED consists of 21,728 pages, with 616,500 word forms and 2,412,000 supporting quotations.

The OED contains a minimum of one citation per century for each entry and at least one usage for every change in meaning. In the first edition, every significant piece of literature from the year 1100 to 1884 was scoured for usages. It is to some extent an homage to one man, for of the 1,827,306 citations listed, almost 2 percent are from the work of William Shakespeare.

As contrasted with *Webster's Third International Dictionary*, the OED is a prescriptive dictionary. Take the two dictionaries' definition of *slang*. The OED judges that slang is "the special vocabulary used by any set of persons of a low or disreputable character," whereas Webster's merely refers to the "language peculiar to a particular group." Ironically, notwithstanding what might be taken as the OED's judgmental orientation, due to the depth and breadth of its scholarship, the OED is the most definitive weapon in countering the false claims of the so-called guardians of English usage.

For example, *Harper's Dictionary of Contemporary Usage* states that *aggravate* originally simply meant "to make worse," as "the fever aggravated his already weakened condition." Based on this supposed "first" meaning of *aggravate*, the popular use of the word to mean "exasperate" is deemed improper. But *Harper's Dictionary* should have consulted the OED. For according to the OED, the first recorded meaning of *aggravate* in 1530 is not to "make worse" but in fact to "make heavy; to load, burden, weigh down."

Language commentator Edwin Newman objects to the "destruction" of the word *rhetoric*. "Rhetoric does not mean . . . exaggeration, or . . . empty phrases. It means — it meant — the effective use of language, and the study of that use." In *Words Fail Us*, author Bob Blackburn also laments the supposed misuse of *rhetoric*. Again, the OED is instructive. One of its definitions of rhetoric is "speech or writing expressed in terms calculated to persuade (often in deprecatory sense), language characterized by artificial or ostentatious expression." The OED shows a usage in this form going back to 1562.

The point is that, for many centuries, writers have been ejaculating jeremiads condemning corruptions of the English language, to little effect. In 1908 grammarian Thomas Lounsbury stated in *The Standard of Usage in English* that "it would save [purists] hours of unnecessary misery were they to make themselves acquainted with the views of prominent men of former times, who felt as did they and talked as foolishly." In a letter written in 1710, writer Jonathan Swift attacked the word "mob" — a shortened form of the term *mobile vulgus*, meaning "the inconstant common people" — with a vengeance. In it he wrote, "I have done my utmost for some years past to stop the progress of 'mobb' and 'banter,' but have been plainly borne down by numbers and betrayed by those who promised to assist me." Swift believed that by the dawn of the twentieth century, all writing from his era would be rendered unintelligible by mutations of vocabulary and grammar. And yet, as Lounsbury points out, "every word of Swift's letter can be understood as easily as it was on the day it was published."

Samuel Coleridge and H. W. Fowler also had their pet peeves. In 1832, Coleridge launched the following assault against the word *talented*. "I regret to see that vile and barbarous vocable 'talented' stealing out of newspapers. . . . Why not shillinged, farthinged, tenpenced, etc.? . . . Most of these pieces of slang come from America." Coleridge was doubly wrong. The first usage of *talented* cited in the OED emanated from England in 1827. And the OED traces the usage of *moneyed* back to the fifteenth century. Keeping up this tradition of acute tonal hypersensitivity, usage doyen Fowler declared that *electrocute* is a "barbarism [that] jars the unhappy Latinists' nerves much more cruelly than the creation denoted jars those of its victim." All the above detested words were virtually entrenched in the language before their detesters were interred. For one period's vulgarisms are merely commonplace to the next generation.

And then there are the myriad "-ize" verbs that have almost convinced some delicate grammarians to "euthanize" themselves. To language writer Edwin Newman, the suffix "-ize is thought to have a businesslike ring . . . or sound technical. What those who use '-ize' overlook is that it is usually unnecessary and always dull . . . and imposes monotony on the language by making so many words sound the same." A panel of experts commissioned by the *Harper Dictionary of Contemporary Usage* characterizes *finalize* as "jargonese," "inelegant," "grotesque."

A few words are in order.

Baptize doesn't sound like *itemize* or *ostracize* to me. And to the claim by some that "-ize" words are jargonish, they have been a fixture of the English language since the sixteenth century. Observe *epitomize* (first used in 1599), *bastardize* (1611), and *colonize* (1622).

Jim Quinn notes in *American Tongue in Cheek*, "If you don't like -ize words, don't use them. But just because you bowdlerize your own language doesn't give you the right to tell the rest of us what to do." Anthony Burgess adds, "When we think we are making an objective judgement about language, we are often merely making a statement about our prejudices."

Rendering definitive statements about language usage is made highly problematic by the constant flux of language. For example, Oxford University Press, in its catalogue promoting the new edition of *Fowler's Dictionary of Modern English Usage*, says that "this masterful revision has been carried out by Robert Burchfield." This comment probably has Fowler turning over in his grave, and not because of an aversion to Burchfield. Fowler never would have accepted this usage of *masterful* and would have insisted upon the word *masterly*. *Masterful* is traditionally defined as "domineering," "vigorous," "imperious," "powerful," whereas *masterly* is defined as "possessing the knowledge or skill of a master." In the mid-1970s, the *Harper Dictionary of Contemporary Usage* asked its "experts" to rule whether *masterful* could be employed in the sense used by Oxford University Press, and 67 percent judged that usage to be improper. The point here is that the word *masterly* is not widely used any more. I suspect even in the 1970s it was a dying word. In the 1990s, any distinction that remained between the two words is clearly dead.

Language experts comprise a distinct breed of cognoscenti. According to Quinn, "other experts have to know something about the subject, and language experts only have to know how to write effectively within the confines of standard journalism." It is never the true linguists, such as Noam Chomsky, Dwight Bolinger, and Robin Lakoff, who are issuing the language fiats.

It is perhaps instructive that the Académie Française has seen fit in its over 350 years of ossified existence to appoint only one linguist to its ranks.

Some of the statements by so-called language guardians display a distinct lack of language knowledge. For example, countless campaigns have been launched against the usage of the word *hopefully*. The sentence "Hopefully, the war will soon be ended" is regarded as erroneous because it doesn't refer to a person doing something in a hopeful manner. But linguist Steven Pinker states, in *The Language Instinct*, that an English adverb does not necessarily have to indicate the manner in which someone performs an action. Like *hopefully*, there are many other adverbs, such as *frankly*, *mercifully*, and *honestly*, that indicate the attitude of the speaker toward the content of the sentence.

All this is not to say that grammar is unimportant. Grammar expresses the logic of a language, and certain rules are indispensable. Verbs should agree with subjects; objects should come after verbs, etc. But grammar is important only insofar as it contributes toward communicating information. Take the following two examples. The mission statement of the corporation I work for states: "We intend to remain the most responsive steel service center. And to grow with our customers . . ." This is poor grammar, not because a sentence starts with the word "and" but because a thought that should have been continuous was chopped up. Call me reactionary, but I also feel that sentences require verbs. Increasingly, writers are dispensing with verbs. Lev Raphael writes in a book review, "So who was Jesus? An educated carpenter committed to upholding the Law . . ." I believe the second sentence should start with the words "He was" to avoid confusion.

We all speak grammatically by virtue of internalizing, in our infancy, the rules of our mother tongue. Take the sentence "The girl drinks milk." No native English-speaker would have to be told that the sentence "Milk the drinks girl" is not proper. Thus, it is fair to say that every language-able person speaks grammatically.

Here, we are talking about descriptive grammar, which describes how people *actually* talk, as opposed to prescriptive grammar, which prescribes how people *ought* to talk.

Prescriptive rules are the ones that were drummed into us throughout our school years, lest we turn into barbarians. It appears, however, that our ennui and suffering might have been in vain. In *The Language Instinct*, linguist Steven Pinker informs us that "most prescriptive rules . . . make no sense on any level. They are bits of folklore that originated for screwball reasons several hundred years ago and have perpetuated themselves ever since."

Heresy, you cry! Surely the entrenched rules of the English language can't be wrong?

Let's examine the evidence. Here are three prescriptive commandments:

1) Thou shalt not split infinitives.
2) Thou shalt not end sentences with a preposition.
3) Thou shalt use whom for objects — never who.

Pinker informs us that it is proper to split infinitives, as in the *Star Trek* mandate "to boldly go where no man has gone before." Ending sentences with prepositions is also proper, and he makes the point by referring to the line attributed to Sir Winston Churchill, "This is the sort of English up with which I will not put." The *who/whom* distinction is a "relic of the English case system only found today in pronouns with distinctions like he/him." Pinker points out that even among pronouns, "the old distinction between subject ye and object you has vanished, leaving you to play both roles . . ." Recently many style guides and dictionaries have started to accept the usage of split infinitives and sentence-ending prepositions.

Compelling evidence, I dare say. What villain is responsible for foisting this elaborate grammatical hoax upon us? It turns out that the villain is the Latin language.

When England emerged as a world power in the Elizabethan era and started to export its language, it had a dilemma. The literati of England saw English as a second-rate language. Since Rome was the paradigmatic successful empire and its language was Latin, it was felt that for English to achieve equivalent political success it would have to be cast into a Latin mold. Linguist Robin Lakoff, in *Talking Power*, says that during the Elizabethan period "a tradition of Latinizing grammars arose . . . remaining influential into the present century."

Bill Bryson, in *The Mother Tongue*, puts it this way: "Making English grammar conform to Latin rules is like asking people to play baseball using the rules of football." Or, as Pinker says, not splitting infinitives "because it isn't done in Latin makes about as much sense as forcing modern residents of England to wear laurels and togas." In Latin, you can't split an infinitive because it is one word; in English it is two words. Caesar's *venire, videre, vincere* in English is rendered as *to come, to see, to conquer.*

Lakoff tells us that, in Latin, prepositions are bound to the nouns they modify, but in English the binding is "less total. . . . So it's less of a problem to move the preposition to the end of the sentence."

"Who do you trust?" I don't think too many of us would say "Whom do you trust?" — it sounds priggish. When we write or when we give a formal speech, we are more likely to employ *whom* lest we be censured for our lack of erudition. As Pinker wryly states, words such as *whom* "serve as shibboleths, differentiating the elite from the rabble."

But fear thee not, ye fellow rabble members, for in good company art thou. Pinker tells us that, as long as prescriptive rules have existed, "speakers have flouted them, spawning identical plaints about the imminent decline of the language. . . . All the best writers in English . . . including Shakespeare, have been among the flagrant flouters."

Part Four

Instrumentality: The Use and Abuse of English

Compared to most other languages, English is concise. A study of the number of syllables required to translate the Gospel According to Mark revealed that English requires 10 percent fewer syllables than German to do so, and 20 percent fewer syllables than French. Also, of the fifty most commonly used English words, not one of them is polysyllabic.

But speaking a language is not the same thing as speaking a language well. Although English has relatively simple grammar, there are many pitfalls — in spelling, pronunciation, and multiplicity of meanings — for the non-native speaker. The English language is also rife with prejudices and issues of political correctness. Anthony Burgess, in *A Mouthful of Air*, says that "knowing the basic words of a language may not be enough. One has to know the strategies."

In this segment, we'll look at some of the strategies of the English language.

22

The meaning of meaning

*I*n June 1997, when the fifteen-member European Union convened in Amsterdam, it fell to Dutch foreign minister Hans Van Mierlo to address the throng of international reporters. To the chagrin of a lone protesting Dutch journalist (and the French nation as a whole), his speech was in the one language that was familiar to the whole assembly: English. The verdict is safely in, and the English language has become the first global lingua franca. The question is, why?

Clearly, the major reason for the preeminence of English lies with the great political and economic clout wielded by the United States, coupled with the pop culture domination of English-speaking countries. There are, however, other attractions. English is brief, relatively free of problematic gender-markers, and possesses far less unnecessary grammar than most languages. It has been calculated that what C. K. Ogden and I. A. Richards have called Basic English comprises approximately

850 words and can be learned within three months.

While learning Basic English may be relatively easy, mastering the myriad strategies of the English language is quite a different matter. Traps abound for the unwary English student. It would seem logical that the words *bough, cough, dough,* and *rough* should all rhyme, yet each word has a distinct pronunciation. Many words, such as *set, ring,* and *strike,* have multitudinous meanings. If someone hears a word that starts with a "b" and rhymes with "pear" or "pare," he has to decipher whether it is *bear* (the animal) or *bear* (tolerate) or perhaps *bare* (naked). Also, the multiplicity of meanings of many common verbs, such as "put," "make," and "go," especially when coupled with other words like "on," "off," and "out," have bewildered many a non-native speaker. Even when the phrase remains constant, the context can totally alter the meaning. For example, the expressions *putting up your dukes, putting up with adversity,* and *putting one up for the night* all express different meanings of the verb "to put."

To complicate matters even more, sometimes the "putting" doesn't even refer to what you "put." Take the following sentence. "Tom was always *putting* balls off the green." Words spelled the same way but carrying different meanings are called heteronyms. If they are pronounced differently (such as *putting,* which can refer to an act of placing or a play in golf), they are referred to as heterophones. The English language is replete with heterophones that are the ultimate pronunciation minefield for the non-native speaker.

In *Crazy English,* wordsmith Richard Lederer concocts the following poem to demonstrate the difficulty posed by English-language heterophones:

Listen, readers, toward me bow.
Be friendly, do not draw the bow.
Please don't try to start a row.
Sit peacefully, all in a row.

Don't squeal like a big, fat sow.
Do not the seeds of discord sow.

Bow (to bend), *row* (an argument), and *sow* (a pig) in lines one, three, and five respectively, all rhyme with the word *cow*. In lines two, four, and six, however, these same words refer to "a weapon," "a line," and "to plant" respectively, and they rhyme with the word "tow."

Many heterophones differ from each other only in the function of the word. This is the case with words such as *house*, which can mean "a dwelling" or "to give shelter," and *pervert*, which can mean "to corrupt" or "one given to sexual perversion." Some heterophones appear to be unconnected but can be traced to a common root. The word *console* can mean "to cheer up" and "a cabinet." Both words are derived from the Latin *consolator*, "one that supports." Similarly *incense*, the noun meaning "an aromatic burnt substance," and *incense*, the verb "to arouse extreme anger," are both derived from the Latin *incendere*, "to set fire to."

The heterophones most likely to prove troublesome are the ones that have no etymological connection but came to be spelled the same way only by linguistic accident. One can usually tell these word pairs apart by the context of the sentence. Sometimes, however, it's not so easy. Take the following manipulated sentences.

"She had a *tear* in her eye but it was repaired surgically."
"Bernard took the *lead* and then the zinc."
"The plant was partly *unionized* and partly ionized."

David Bergeron, in an article on heteronyms and heterophones in *English Today*, displays their ambiguity in the following heterophonic thought: "Surely *agape* could not be a foreigner's emotion as he or she becomes frustrated with our *supply* textured English words . . ." The context of the sentence leads even the seasoned English reader to interpret the italicized heterophonic words in the wrong manner until the whole sentence has been integrated and he can switch to the correct heterophonic option.

With the ever-changing nature of English, who knows what hitherto unknown heterophones are lurking? *Despot* may become the action of a dry cleaner, and *resin* could be something you do to double the pleasure. Heterophonic chaos may reign in the next millennium. Bergeron predicts that, as the English language solidifies its hegemonic position, "linguistic anglicizing of cultural concepts and tangible items previously unnamed in English may result in an explosion of heteronyms over the next centuries."

Now that you are totally demoralized by the complexity of the English language, I've prepared a postmodern word puzzle guaranteed to boost your self-esteem.

1) *sanction* (verb) means:
   (a) to forbid (b) to permit
2) *cleave* means:
   (a) to split apart (b) to adhere
3) Which of these two words means to disentangle?:
   (a) ravel (b) unravel
4) Which of these two words means "capable of burning"?:
   (a) flammable (b) inflammable

Regardless of your answers, you are correct. Both *sanction* and *cleave* carry two, opposing meanings. *Flammable* means the same as *inflammable*, and *ravel* can mean the same as *unravel*. *Ravel* can also mean "to tangle" as well as "to disentangle," apparently because as the threads become unwoven their ends become tangled. Confused? Let me try to unravel this mystery.

In the case of the two senses of *cleave*, there is a simple explanation. *Cleave*, "to split," descends from the Old English *cleofan*, whereas *cleave*, "to adhere," is derived from the Old English *cli-fian*. Over time, both words with opposite meanings came to be spelled identically.

Words are constantly acquiring additional senses or altogether new meanings, sometimes diametrically opposed to their original sense. For example, *brave* originally implied cowardice, as in *bravado*, and *awful* originally meant "inspiring awe." It came to mean "bad" because what inspires awe is frightening, and what is frightening is usually thought of as being bad.

Usually when a word acquires a sense diametrically opposite to its original meaning, the first sense dies out. This is what happened to the word *egregious*. It came into the language in the sixteenth century and meant "prominent," but it soon also acquired the contradictory sense of being "conspicuously bad." By the nineteenth century, its former positive sense had faded away.

However, contradictory meanings can coexist. Take the word *sanction*. The opposite meaning arises from the legal sense of ordination, which implies the granting of penalties as well as the granting of rights.

In *The Making of English*, Henry Bradley, onetime editor of *The Oxford English Dictionary*, explains the process whereby both *fast* and *fine* acquired contradictory meanings: "The primary sense of 'fast' is 'firm,' immovable." But the notion of firmness, which appears in the expression *to stand fast*, was developed by an easy transition, into that of strength and unwavering persistence of movement. Hence it became possible to speak of *running fast*. In the case of *fine*, he explains that its original sense is of being "highly finished." The original sense of being highly finished extended in two directions. When intricacy was admired, the sense of *fine* became "small," but when admiration was shown for growth, *fine* acquired the sense of "large."

In *Declining Grammar*, Dennis Baron points out that the fear of ambiguity can actually lead to some lexical paradoxes. *Inflammable* came into the language in the seventeenth century with the meaning "that which can be inflamed." By the nineteenth century, however, concerns were raised that someone might start a fire by mistaking *inflammable* for *non-flammable*, and thus the word *flammable* was born in 1813.

Literally, employed to mean "figuratively," is the bête noire of language critics. The position of *Harper's Dictionary of Contemporary Usage* is that "if you say, 'He literally hit the ceiling' when you describe a very angry man, you are saying that he struck the plaster overhead." Frederick Crews and Sandra Schor concur in *The Borzoi Handbook for Writers*, saying that "If you write, 'I literally died laughing,' you must be writing from beyond the grave."

To me, 'tis much ado about nothing. In both cases, it is obvious that the context is metaphoric. In any case, like it or not, this paradoxical use of *literally* is not going to disappear. What should be avoided, however, are ambiguous statements such as "He was literally starving," where the inherent sense is not obvious.

Language purists take heart. Baron says that "intensifiers such as 'really' and 'truly' eventually lose their intensity and become candidates for replacement. So . . . speakers and writers of English will insist on using 'literally' in its new sense only until something better comes along."

Other lexical contradictions, however, are not about to disappear. The double meanings of *dust* — "to sprinkle with dust" or "to remove it" — have coexisted since the sixteenth century. *Scan*, whose only meaning used to be "to examine closely," can now also mean "to skim." And the same fate has befallen *peruse*. As much as one would like, one *literally* cannot escape confusion.

23

Sex, lex, and the law

"I have never had sexual relations with Monica Lewinsky."
— BILL CLINTON IN A JANUARY 17, 1998, DEPOSITION

*"I want to say one thing to the American people. . . . I did not
have sexual relations with that woman, Miss Lewinsky."*
— BILL CLINTON SPEAKING TO REPORTERS, JANUARY 26, 1998

*P*resident Clinton, in his August 17, 1998, "mea culpa," stated that he'd had a "relationship that was not appropriate," that he was guilty of a "critical lapse of judgment," and that he'd "misled people, including even my wife." Yet he claimed that his denial of having sexual relations with Monica Lewinsky at the January 17 deposition was "legally accurate." Is this possible? Let us study the question from a semantic perspective.

According to an article in *The New York Times*, "there is no generic legal definition of sexual relations, the description of which depends on the context of the case — civil or criminal, sexual harassment or rape — and the specific statutes where the case resides."

The Paula Jones lawsuit, however, provides us with a precise definition of "sexual relations": "Contact with the genitalia, anus, groin, breast, inner thigh or buttocks of any person with an intent to arouse or gratify the sexual desire of any person."

Clinton is thus claiming that he did not establish contact with any of the six aforementioned private parts. So whereas Ms. Lewinsky made contact with the first item in the list of six, it can be argued, in a convoluted fashion, that she had "sexual relations" with President Clinton but Clinton, by virtue of being a totally passive recipient, did not have sexual relations with Ms. Lewinsky. Putting it another way, in the sentence "Monica contacted Bill sexually," Monica is the sexual subject, Bill is the sexual object. It would appear that the biblical counsel "it is more blessed to give than to receive" does not apply at grand jury deliberations.

Only one dictionary, *Webster's Ninth New Collegiate Dictionary*, defines *sexual relations*, albeit tersely, as "coitus." The term was absent from over ten other dictionaries.

But let us expand our lexical horizons. We will assume that President Clinton was the recipient of an act of oral sex from the aforementioned White House intern. This being the case, can we say whether he engaged in *sexual intercourse*? Let us examine the lexical evidence.

One of the definitions for *sexual intercourse* in *Webster's Third New International Dictionary* is "genital contact between individuals other than penetration of the vagina by the penis." Clearly, the individuals in the Oval Office established contact. *Webster's Third* verdict: GUILTY.

The American Heritage Dictionary proves to be the dictionary of choice among partygoers. It defines *sexual intercourse* as "intercourse by two or more individuals involving genital stimulation." Assuming Exhibit B (the genetic material) found on Exhibit A (the blue Gap dress) belongs to the President, there definitely was stimulation. *American Heritage* verdict: GUILTY.

The Random House *Dictionary of the English Language* defines *sexual intercourse* as "genital contact, especially the insertion of the penis into the vagina followed by orgasm." While it appears the President climaxed, nothing was inserted. *Random House* verdict: NOT GUILTY.

Chambers Dictionary defines *sexual intercourse* as "the uniting of sexual organs, especially involving insertion of the male penis into the female vagina and the release of sperm." One wonders why Chambers felt it necessary to specify "male penis" and "female vagina." In any case, vis-à-vis the President, there was no insertion. *Chambers* verdict: NOT GUILTY.

The Concise Oxford English Dictionary defines *sexual intercourse* as "physical contact between individuals involving sexual stimulation of the genitals" and states that there is usually an "ejaculation of semen." *Concise Oxford* verdict: GUILTY (on both counts).

The Oxford English Dictionary is helpful in providing historical usages of the expression *having sex*. From D. H. Lawrence's 1929 *Pansies*, a book of poetry, we have "If you want to have sex, you've got to trust"; S. Kauffmann's *Philanderers* in 1952 provides "Her arms went round his neck and his hand rested on her waist, and they had a brief moment of friendship before the sex began," and from the BBC's *The Listener* in 1962, we have "Why wasn't Bond 'more tender' in his love-making? Why did he just 'have sex' and disappear?"

Unfortunately, in none of these three citations is there any reference to the particular act Ms. Lewinsky is purported to have performed. Ergo, *Oxford English Dictionary* verdict: NOT GUILTY, by virtue of lack of evidence.

How do Canadian dictionaries judge the President? In the true Canadian spirit, it's a split decision. *The Canadian Oxford Dictionary* makes reference to "genital contact" in its definition of *sexual intercourse*. *Canadian Oxford Dictionary* verdict: GUILTY. *Gage Canadian Dictionary*, on the other hand, refers to the joining of "sexual organs." *Gage* verdict: NOT GUILTY.

Final tabulations result in a four-four deadlock on whether *sexual intercourse* occurred. The lexical jury is still out on William Jefferson Clinton.

24

Reaching out and touching someone is not P.C.

*W*riting in 1991, Rosalie Maggio in *The Dictionary of Bias-Free Usage* remarked that "sexual harassment was not a term anyone used twenty years ago; today we have laws against it." The term *sexual harassment* was born in 1975. This is not to say that people weren't harassed sexually prior to 1975; there just wasn't a term to describe it.

What exactly is *sexual harassment* and how is it defined in Canada? *Gage Canadian Dictionary* defines it as "unwelcome sexual advance, sexual comments, etc. directed towards someone by a fellow employee, an employer, or a superior, especially if compliance constitutes a form of blackmail." I checked with some local universities to see how they defined the term. The definition by Montreal's Concordia University refers to "unwelcome sexual invitations or requests, demands for sexual favors or unwelcome and repeated innuendoes . . ." At McGill University, "sexual harassment is a display of sexual attention towards another individual . . . of a nature which may reasonably be considered to be vexatious or abusive."

My preferred definition is McGill's, as it avoids the indefinable words "unwanted" or "unwelcome." The attention that is unwanted and unwelcome to one person may be desired by another.

Just as the universe has been expanding in recent years, so have the definitions of sexual harassment. Kate Roiphe, in *The Morning After*, relates that when she attended Princeton University in the late 1980s the operative definition of sexual harassment was "unwanted sexual attention that makes a person feel uncomfortable." According to a Princeton student manual, it might result from a "conscious or unconscious action and can be subtle or blatant and can include whistling . . . sexual innuendo and other suggestive or offensive or derogatory comments, humor and jokes about sex." Holding people responsible for "unconscious actions" is particularly troubling. To do so is a thinly veiled attempt at thought control.

Unfortunately, this Kafkaesque mind-set has also infected Canadian universities. Carole Oliver relates, in a 1995 article in *The Globe and Mail*, how her twenty-one-year-old son was dropped as a lecturer at Ottawa's Carleton University because of an unspecified complaint from a female student. Oliver's inquiry to an official met with the following incredible reply: "It is sufficient for one student to say to another 'I feel uncomfortable when so and so is in the room with me' and the concern will automatically be acted upon, with no attempt to establish innocence or guilt."

At Princeton, Roiphe says that counselors would tell students, "if you *feel* sexually harassed, you *were* sexually harassed." At Princeton's Terrace Club, "the refuge of fashionable left-leaning . . . undergraduates, a sign proclaimed: 'What constitutes sexual harassment . . . is to be defined by the person harassed and his/her own feelings of being threatened or compromised.'" Due to this kind of skewed reasoning, university administrators have sometimes sacrificed professional careers upon the altar of so-called "political correctness."

Novelist Francine Prose related in a 1995 *New York Times* article that a male academic colleague was charged with sexual harassment for his "salty language used outside the classroom at graduate-student parties." At his hearing, Prose says, "there was much talk of protecting women from blunt mention of sex. Victorian damsels in distress, they used 19th century language: they had been 'shattered' by his rude, 'brutish' behavior." She later opines, "Are these the modern women feminists had in mind? Victorian girls, Puritan girls, crusading against dirty thoughts and loose speech."

Definitions of sexual harassment have been blurred by university discussions that refer to "a poisoned environment" and "patterns of intimidation." In fact, at McGill University there are those who would like to see the definition of sexual harassment expanded to include such criteria.

There is, however, an extreme danger in doing so. Francine Prose concludes her article by reminding us of the "swift ease with which our rights can simply crumble away, gathering momentum as the erosion process begins — until human rights and women's rights are subjects too salty to mention."

By the way, if you labor in a non-academic sphere, as I do, don't feel you're immune from the above. I recently received from an American client a copy of the company's sexual harassment policy. I was instructed to forward it to any employee that might have contact with them, "i.e., truck drivers, salesmen, etc." I was told by an employee of this company that its policy was formulated because, according to the Equal Employment Opportunity Commission in the United States, something might be deemed to be sexual harassment and illegal if it "has the purpose or effect of unreasonably interfering with an individual's work performance or creating an intimidating, hostile or offensive working environment."

So unless you work for Ma Bell, your motto should not be "Reach out and touch someone."

25

One woman's euphemism is another woman's dysphemism

*T*he twentieth century has provided us with some horrific euphemisms, from *concentration camp* to *ethnic cleansing*. George Orwell, in his famous essay "Politics and the English Language," states that euphemism is "designed to make lies sound truthful and murder respectable, and to give appearance of solidity to pure wind." In 1978, a National Airlines 727 airplane crashed while attempting to land in Pensacola, Florida, killing three of its fifty-two passengers. As a result of this accident, National made an after-tax profit of $1.7 million, which, it explained in its annual report, was due to "the involuntary conversion of a 727."

To someone who has lost his job it is small consolation to hear that it's a result of *downsizing*, *right sizing*, or being *excessed*. Nor does he want to hear that he's been given a *career-change opportunity*. There is even an acronym, *RIF (reduction in force)*, that allows the ex-employee to say "I was riffed" rather than admit he was fired.

This is only half the tale about euphemisms. In sugarcoating the truth, euphemisms can soothe. For example, to say that your grandfather has *passed away* or that your aunt has become *absentminded* in her old age is less brutal than using the words *dead* and *senile*. And for certain subjects, such as sex, euphemisms are essential. If we didn't have them, we would have to choose between using clinical language — such as "genitalia" and "reproductive organs" — or the litany of four-letter words.

Robert Burchfield, onetime editor of *The Oxford English Dictionary*, once mused that "a language without euphemism would be a defective instrument of communication." Language is not value-neutral, and all eras have used euphemisms to ameliorate and to disparage, to camouflage taboos, and to make the unseemly seemly.

Frequently euphemisms come to be too closely associated with what they have replaced, so that fresher euphemisms must be invented. A *cemetery* was originally a euphemism to replace "burial ground." Literally, a cemetery is a "sleeping place." Nowadays, for some people, it no longer provides the comfortable distance from the original idea, and so *cemetery* has been replaced by *memorial park*. A "toilet" used to be the appropriate place where one retreated from polite company, but not any longer. Even the term *bathroom* seems too lurid for many and has been replaced by the less active-sounding *restroom*. You won't find the word *retarded* included in modern dictionaries of euphemisms, but originally the word was used euphemistically as a substitute for the term "idiot."

Euphemisms are by their nature transitory and, if undressed, they can turn into their opposites, *dysphemisms*. In *Euphemism & Dysphemism*, Keith Allan and Kate Burridge define a dysphemism as "an expression with connotations that are offensive either about the denotatum or to the audience, or both, and is substituted for a neutral or euphemistic expression for just that reason." They tell us that dysphemisms are used when "talking about our opponents, things we show disapproval of, and things one wishes to downgrade, characteristic of political groups, feminists speaking about men and misogynists talking about women." So, a troublesome mother-in-law might become "the old battle-ax," an unloved wife "my ball-and-chain," or a domineering employer "the big boss."

It can be problematic, however, telling dysphemisms and euphemisms apart. Normally, the word *lady* is used in a complimentary fashion, but if it is used derisively it becomes dysphemistic. Similarly, the neutral word *girl* can be used dysphemistically to imply wanton behavior or low social status. British writer Robert M. Adams relates the anecdote of attending a concert in Japan, which he disliked immensely. At the intermission, the Japanese couple accompanying him asked him how he was enjoying the concert. He replied hesitatingly that he found the concert "'very melancholy and a bit monotonous.' They exclaimed, 'Melancholy and monotonous, just so!' And it was clear I could not have paid a higher tribute." To complicate matters even further, we have euphemistic dysphemisms, such as *sugar!* (to replace a similar-sounding vulgarity), and dysphemistic euphemisms, such as *the curse* (for menstruation).

The need for a euphemism is often highly subjective. I was once assured by a fellow worker that he never refers to me as a "Jew" but as a *Jewish person.* I attempted to explain to him that the term "Jew" was value-neutral, but I don't think I convinced him. For many years, the terms *colored, Afro-American,* and *Negro* served in a sense as euphemisms for the word "black." Hugh Rawson says that the word *Negro* has alternately served as a "euphemism for 'nigger' and sometimes as a dysphemism for 'black.'" He relates that long after black Americans had indicated their preference for being called "blacks," the St. Louis *Globe* insisted on calling them "Negroes," in a dysphemistic fashion.

William Safire, in *Watch Your Language*, says that comedian and activist Dick Gregory in his book *Nigger* "bit down hard on a painful slur turning it to his advantage." When used among blacks to each other in casual conversation, the term *nigger* is not used insultingly but can be a term of endearment. There is no unanimity concerning this usage in the black community, however. Earl Ofari Hutchinson, in *The Assassination of the Black Male Image*, asserts that "the word 'nigger' — no matter who uses it or how it is used — remains the most hurtful and enduring symbol of black oppression."

Traditionally, the homosexual community has favored highly euphemistic language, such as *coming out of the closet*, *cruising*, and *gay*. Increasingly, however, seemingly dysphemistic words such as *fairy*, *queen*, and *queer* are being worn as a badge of honor. Usage of the word *queer* in a neutral sense is starting to become commonplace in *straight* circles.

Perhaps this will start a trend in the new millennium. As the saying goes, "sticks and stones may break your bones, but names will never hurt you" — especially if the pejorative sense of those names can be neutralized.

26

Acronynms are also useful for euphemizing and satirizing

L ooking for a space-saver? Try acronyms and initialisms. Take the following two sentences: "By taking *AZT*, the *HIV* patient forestalled getting *AIDS* and no *DNA* changes occurred"; "Despite being exposed to *DDT* and *LSD*, his level of *ACTH* didn't drop." In the first sentence, having to employ the words "azidothymidine," "human immunodeficiency virus," "acquired immune deficiency syndrome," and "deoxyribonucleic acid" would have resulted in a sentence more than twice as long. And though the second sentence is practically gibberish, at least by using acronyms instead of the words "dichlorodiphenyl-trichloroethane," "lysergic acid diethylamide," and "adreno-corticotropic hormone," the gibberish has been reduced by 57.4 percent.

Particularly in the technical world, acronyms are indispensable because they save time in expressing concepts. And by expressing the written word in less space, they are also ecologically proper. Less space means less paper, hence more trees.

Acronyms can be divided into two groups: true acronyms, such as *NATO*, can be pronounced as words, and initialisms, such as *CBC*, are abbreviations that consist of the initial letters of a series of words. Not all acronyms are obvious, and many words that enjoy an acronymic heritage are not fully appreciated. Some examples are *scuba* (self-contained underwater breathing apparatus), *radar* (radio detecting and ranging), *laser* (light amplification by stimulated emission of radiation), *sonar* (sound navigation ranging), and *modem* (modulator/demodulator).

Acronyms have given rise to many spurious etymologies. For example, it is commonly believed that the word *tip* is an acronym for "to insure promptness." *Cop* is said to be an acronym for "constable on patrol." *Posh* is reported to be an acronym for "port out, starboard home." All these origins, however, are merely folkloric. A *cop* is someone who etymologically "cops" (grabs) a robber, and there is no definitive etymology for either *posh* or *tip*.

Although used primarily to achieve brevity, acronyms are sometimes rendered in the interests of gentility. Terms such as *BS*, *SOB*, and *snafu* serve as euphemisms by camouflaging taboo words and phrases. The standard response to stupid questions on electronic bulletin boards is *RTFM*. It stands for "Read the f — — ing manual."

Creating a code is just as enjoyable as breaking one. And using acronyms as the building block of the code has been the preferred construction material of many a wag.

Acronyms are a timesaving tool of disparagement. In the dialect of acronyms, the legal degree *LLD* becomes "License to Lie Damnably"; *TLC* becomes "Total Lack of Concern"; *CIA* becomes "Caught In the Act"; and *OPEC* becomes "Oil People Enjoying Cadillacs."

Cars have long been a favorite target for acronymic satire. In alphabetical order, the hidden meaning of various automobile names is revealed:

AUDI: Accelerates Under Demonic Influence
BMW: Bus, Metro, Walk
BUICK: Big, Ugly Indestructible Car Killer
CHEVROLET: Can Hear Every Valve Rattle On Long
   Extended Trips
FIAT: Failure in Italian Automotive Technology (it actually
   stands for Fabbrica Italiana Automobili Torino).
FORD: (in reverse order) Driver Returns On Foot
HYUNDAI: Hope You Understand Nothing's Drivable And
   Inexpensive
OLDSMOBILE: Old Ladies Driving Slowly Make Others
   Behind Infuriatingly Late Everyday
VOLVO: Very Odd-Looking Vehicular Object

Airlines have also enjoyed the acronymic wrath. Observe ALI-TALIA: "Always Late In Takeoffs And Landings In Airport"; DELTA: "Don't Ever Leave The Airport"; and EL AL: "Embarks Late, Arrives Late."

Nowhere are acronyms more prevalent than in the field of computers. We are assailed by countless acronyms such as *CD-ROM* (compact disc-read only memory), *MIPS* (millions of instructions per second), and *WYSIWYG* (what you see is what you get).

Lately, bogus computer acronyms have supplanted car acronyms as the favorite forum for wordsmiths. The Internet is replete with sites that sport inventive computer acronyms. Here is a sampling:

APPLE: Arrogance Produces Profit-Losing Enterprise
BASIC: Bill's Attempt to Seize Industry Control
CD-ROM: Consumer Device Rendered Obsolete in Months
DOS: Defective Operating System

IBM: I Blame Microsoft

MACINTOSH: Most Applications Crash; If Not The
    Operating System Hangs

MICROSOFT: Most Intelligent Customers Realize Our
    Software Only Fools Teenagers

PENTIUM: Produces Erroneous Numbers Through Incorrect
    Understanding of Mathematics

WINDOWS: Will Install Needless Data On Whole System

WWW: World Wide Wait

BTW (by the way), expect to see even more acronyms in
the future. *B/c* (because), there are many people, like me, with
mediocre keyboard skills communicating via computers. *IMHO*
(in my humble opinion), this type of sentence will become more
common *FYI* (for your information) needs.

27

Biblical animals have fallen from grace

*"Behold, thy King cometh unto thee, meek, and sitting
upon an* ass.*"* — MATTHEW 21:5

*"The high hills are a refuge for the wild goats; and the
rocks for the* conies.*"* — PSALM 104:18

"The cock *shall not crow this day, before that thou shalt thrice
deny that thou knowest me."* — LUKE 22:34

*A*ll the animals noted above are featured in the King James Version of the Bible, which was completed in 1614. Over time, however, some animal names became tainted and had to be replaced: *ass* by donkey, *coney* by rabbit, and *cock* by rooster.

St. Matthew informs us that "many that are first shall be last." Ironically, *arse* has become a euphemism for itself, and in the process it has sullied our first biblical animal. *Arse* is defined by *The Oxford English Dictionary* (OED) as "the fundament, buttocks, posteriors, or rump of an animal," and its first citation is from the year 1000. It coexisted with the animal *ass*, whose first citation in the OED is also from 1000.

But by the eighteenth century the word *ass* had been expunged from genteel society. What force kicked the ass from its lexicological throne?

In many languages the letter "r" stops being pronounced when it precedes the letter "s." This occurred in many places in

England as well as in parts of New England and the southern United States. Thus *burst* could be pronounced as "bust," *horse* as "hoss," *curse* as "cuss," and of course *arse* as "ass."

It just would not do for a *lass* to rhyme with the newly pronounced *arse*, and it became proper to avoid using the animal name around 1760. Hugh Rawson relates in his *Dictionary of Euphemism and Other Doubletalk* that "pre-Victorians became nervous about calling the barnyard critter, the ass, by its rightful name, because the three-letter word sounded like the bad four-letter one when the 'r' was dropped." Enter *donkey*.

But *donkey* did not emerge as the definitive ass substitute immediately. For about fifty years the word *neddy*, a diminutive for the name Edward, was used just as frequently, and it wasn't until 1830 that *donkey* was ensconced as the heir apparent. The usual etymological explanation of *donkey* is that it descends from the word "dun," meaning brownish gray, and that the "k" was added to make it rhyme with "monkey," which it did originally.

Rawson informs us that the word *rabbit* originally applied only "to the young of the long-eared Lepus cunicula." The definitive word for the adult of this species was *cony*, which was also spelled *coney* and *cunny*, and it rhymed with "honey." Herein lies the root of why the word became improper. Rawson tells us that *cony* was also "a term of endearment for a woman and a reference to her most PRIVATE PART."

Thus the word *cony*, which referred to the adult of the species, was deemed to have too much of an "adult" sense, and it was replaced in the nineteenth century by the word *rabbit*. There still remained the problem of what to do when reading the Bible. In 1836, Benjamin H. Smart found a solution. The OED tells us that for "solemn reading" Smart ordained that what previously rhymed with "honey" would henceforth rhyme with "bony."

Not only has the word *cock* been unceremoniously ousted by *rooster*, many words featuring *cock* have been bowdlerized. Apricots were once *apricocks* or *apricox*, haystacks were originally *haycocks*, and weathervanes were once *weathercocks*. Even people's names were subject to the expunging of *cocks*. Nineteenth-century author Louisa May Alcott was so surnamed because her father had changed the family name from Alcox. Canadian author T. C. Haliburton was probably having sport, however, in his 1844 novel *Sam Slick*, when he had a young man tell a young woman that her brother had become not a *coxswain* in the navy, but a *rooster-swain*.

The word *cock* is probably of onomatopoeic origin, imitative of the male fowl's "cockadoodledoo" call. In French, this becomes *coquerico* and in German *kikeriki*. *Cock* echoes similar words in other languages, notably the Old Norse *kokkr* and the medieval Latin *coccus*.

Alas, Wilfred Funk, in *Word Origins*, relates that the proud *cock* was to develop "figurative associations." Shakespeare had more in mind than the bearing of arms in *Henry V* when Pistol yells at Nym: "Pistol's cock is up." Funk delicately tells us in his 1950 book that when *cock*'s allusions "became widely enough known among men and boys the term grew indecent and unspeakable and remains in men's language only." Enter *rooster*.

The first citation of *rooster* in the OED is an American reference from 1772. The word was still unusual enough in England fifty years later that James Flint, in his 1822 *Letters from America*, had to explain to British readers that "rooster, or he-bird, is the male of the hen."

So in place of the wonderfully rich word *cock*, we have the mediocre word *rooster* (i.e., he who roosts) as the definitive word for this animal. And unlike Jesus, who may have been denied three times by Peter, we are denied three proud biblical words: *ass*, *cony*, and *cock*.

The degradation process, however, is not restricted to animal words.

In 1989 freelance journalist Harry Flemming wrote in *Atlantic Insight* that after having been incarcerated for eleven years for a murder he did not commit, Donald Marshall Jr. "accepted the government's niggardly offer of $270,000."

This comment drew the ire of one Gillian D. Butler, then Chief Adjudicator of the Human Rights Commission of the Newfoundland Justice Department. Ms. Butler felt that the magazine should have been "sensitive enough to human rights issues to have refused to publish the article in this form" and added indignantly that "surely, [Blacks] are entitled to protection from discrimination."

One of the corollaries of semantic sensitivity is that it engenders semantic hypersensitivity, if not outright silliness. The word *niggardly* is no more racist because of its sound than the word *menstruate* is sexist because its first three letters are "men." *Niggardly*, which derives from the Norwegian *gnigga*, means "stingy"; in 1374 Chaucer writes in *Troilus and Criseyde*, "So parfaite joye may no negarde have," to refer to the joy denied to a miser.

Ms. Butler's foible reminds me of an anecdote related by a friend. During a family dinner, he swallowed hard and asked, "Ma, don't you ever use condiments?" This question drew the wrath of his mother who replied, "Normie, don't talk dirty at the dinner table!"

Words such as *condiments* and *niggardly*, which conjure up "condom" and a racial epithet respectively, were labeled "suggestibles" by John Ellison Kahn in the language journal *Verbatim*. Other suggestibles include the word *fatuous*, which suggests the word "fat," and homonym-like words such as *titter, hoary,* and *pith*, if you lisp. He calls this tendency of seeing alternate meanings to a word as "polysemania," which he defines as "an abnormal awareness of possible ambiguity; an uncontrollable tendency to bring to mind the inappropriate or unintended sense of a word in any context."

Kahn informs us that polysemania is not a new phenomenon and that "Hamlet and Othello were victims of it in their own way. Pathological punsters have no doubt always plagued polite society, and willful verbal misunderstandings have always ruined human relationships." For some obsessive folks, however, any word can evoke such a possible double entendre. The extreme polysemaniac is "afflicted by a hysterical muteness, having arrived at the mad (and obvious) intuition that almost any utterance is susceptible of a faulty interpretation." (This is mostly a characteristic of many of us who possess the Y chromosome and cannot conjure words like the name of the planet Uranus without secretly chuckling.)

When the sound of a word reminds us of another word, the sense of that word invariably becomes tainted. The Old English word for "illness" was *adl*, but since it reminded people of the word *adela*, which meant dirt, it was replaced by the euphemistic *disease* in the fourteenth century.

Words also acquire a semantic taint in other ways. For example, the value attached to the meaning of a word can be determined by a dominant social group. Thus, the word *vulgar* originally meant only that one was not lucky enough to have been born a member of the upper classes, and did not suggest any lasciviousness. *Villain* had no dastardly connotation but merely referred to a farm servant.

Words with negative connotations that start off as genderless tend to become the property of women; the word *harlot* originally meant "beggar" or "tramp," and acquired the sense of "prostitute" only in the fifteenth century. And since right-handedness is dominant, the original Old English word for left, *winestra* (which came from the Latin *sinistra*, for "left hand"), came to mean evil in the form of *sinister*.

Historical context can also give a word a certain tinge. If you look up the word *appeasement* in the dictionary it is likely to show a meaning of "to bring to a state of peace." In the wake of pre–World War II Munich, it has acquired the sense of "trying to buy off an aggressor." In light of similar events in World War II, I will always see the word *collaboration* tainted with cowardice, rather than as a synonym for cooperation. I suspect that the

Clinton-Lewinsky tryst might taint the word *intern*.

Once the sense of a word has been coopted, it is almost impossible to use the word in its original sense without being aware of the usurped meaning. It's difficult to hear the verse "don we now our *gay* apparel" without conjuring up an image of cross-dressers. Likewise, I suspect, the word *queer* is used rarely today in its original sense of "peculiar."

English polysemania is so virulent that it can infect other languages. Peter Farb, in *Word Play*, tells us that "the Creek Indians of Oklahoma avoid their words *fakki*, 'earth,' and *apissi*, 'fat,' because of their resemblance to tabooed English words." Similarly, Farb tells us that in the Nootka Indian language of Vancouver Island, the word for female genitalia so closely resembles the word *such* that "teachers find it very difficult to convince their students to utter the English word in class."

So enjoy your words while you can, for you never know when they will fall from grace.

28

The seven deadly sins are "in" and proud of it

"*We profited* from their misfortune — no, let me rephrase that, it sounds too mercantile. We *benefited* — no, that's not right — we have *gained an advantage* — no! — well, you know what I'm trying to say." A friend was relating to me a discussion she heard recently during a religious service. She said the speaker was trying to convey a sense of spiritual accomplishment but was stymied by the seemingly capitalistic nature of the verbs he employed.

Moneyed words are so central to our lives that any verb our hapless discussant used to communicate a sense of acquisition would have had the capitalist taint he was trying to eschew. The words *obtain*, *earn*, and *procure* carry the same connotation. In the long history of the English language, this mercantile sense wasn't always prevalent. But with the demise of feudalism and the ability of the common man to sell his labor freely, the need for new terms to reflect the new economic realities arose.

Usually, when a new field of endeavor arises, a jargon comes along with it. This specialized vocabulary serves as a shibboleth to a certain group and thus helps demarcate those who should be included in the select group and those who should be excluded. This did not happen, however, with words in the economic sphere. The vocabulary of capitalism is laced with words from other domains. Words like *account, budget, business, company, consumption, demand, duty, income, interest, market, pay,* and *purchase* all existed previously and were adapted to describe the new economic system. Probably the reason a selective vocabulary didn't develop was because of the centrality of these words to everyone's existence.

Many of these words once had radically different meanings. For example, when you *paid* a creditor, you weren't paying him, rather you were "pacifying" him. *Purchase* originally meant "to take by force." In Old French, *un enfant de perchas* was a term for a bastard; the implication is that a bastard is the product of a rape.

The end of feudalism necessitated new interpretations of words. *Service* was no longer an obligation, and many of the words to describe service and servants became pejorative terms. For example, a *knave* was originally just a term for a lower-class male child, and a *lackey* was a term for a footsoldier. Conversely, words that denoted a high status, like *noble* and *gentle*, came to possess a higher moral value.

With the ability to sell one's labor freely, words began to take on new connotations. Originally *fortune* referred only to chance; it didn't develop its sense of "great wealth" until the end of the sixteenth century. The point is that *fortune* was no longer seen as being controlled by others but now could be controlled by an individual.

Some words originally had a communal rather than an individual sense. *Wealth* once had the sense of communal wellness still displayed in the word *commonwealth*. By the sixteenth century it was used to describe an abundance, but it was not until the eighteenth century that it obtained its primary association with money. *Profit* was also originally associated with a community as opposed to an individual, but the focus changed with the growing tide of capitalism. Just as the "common weal" gave way to private wealth, communal profit gave way to individual profit.

M. M. Poston, in *The Medieval Economy and Society*, points out that profit and economic expansion in feudal days was inhibited by the concept of a "just price." This price was more than an injunction against excessive profit. Since the Church was essentially a conservative institution dedicated to preserving the status quo, "[i]t linked the price system with the divinely ordained structure of society, by defining a 'just' price as that which would yield the makers of goods and their sellers sufficient income to maintain them in their respective social ranks."

With the movement to a more secular society, equality first became an assumption, and then an inherent right of all men. According to Raymond Williams, in *Keywords*, *equality* is first used in the fifteenth century in reference to physical quantities, and in the sixteenth century to refer to equivalence of rank. The suggestion of "freedom" is thus one that is limited to the aristocracy. It is only with the French and American Revolutions that the term acquires a universal sense.

The advent of capitalism led to the amelioration of many words. In feudal times, to be *free* and *frank* implied only that one was not bound to a master. *Generous* suggested a noble lineage and not nobility of spirit, and, according to the OED, "'liberal' was originally the distinctive epithet of those arts and sciences that were considered worthy of a free man."

This is not to imply that our more secular society is a morally superior one. Geoffrey Hughes, in *Words in Time*, postulates that the seven deadly sins — pride, wrath, envy, lust, gluttony, avarice, and sloth — are generally all seen, if not as virtues, then as neutral concepts. Pride is seen in a positive light, vanity has been ameliorated by terms like *vanity case*, and anger is seen as often justified. Envy and avarice are concomitant with capitalism, and lust, gluttony, and sloth are seen as facets of the "good life." No word better sums up this dramatic shift than the word *luxury*. In the fourteenth century, it had the sense of "lasciviousness" or "lust." By the seventeenth century, it had acquired a sense of habitual use of what is choice or costly, and it wasn't until the nineteenth century that it obtained its modern sense of contributing to sumptuous living.

But who knows? Now that the conspicuous consumption of capitalism is endangering our resource-depleted planet, perhaps one day *luxury* will regain its rapacious sense.

For goodness' sake, let's put the sin back in the Seven Deadlies!

29

By God! Lefties are all right

*A*nd the nominees for the group most disparaged by the English language are:

A) Women: Invariably, when a term applies to women a pejorative hue appears. Compare *mistress* to *mister*, *governess* to *governor*, *majorette* to *major*, and *spinster* to *bachelor*. There are, however, many terms for women, such as *mother*, *sister*, *lady*, that have positive connotations, and scores of others that are value-neutral.

B) Blacks: Many "black" words have negative connotations, such as *blackmail*, *black mark*, *black market*, *blackball*, *black sheep*, *black eye*, and *denigrate*. Yet, there are many "black" terms such as *black book* and *blackbird* that are neutral, and even some "black" terms, such as *black tie*, *black belt*, and *in the black*, that have positive connotations.

My vote for the group most castigated by the English language goes to that sinister cabal who, by definition, can do no right:

C) Left-handed people.

Let's examine the evidence. The august *Oxford English Dictionary* (OED) defines *left* as follows: "Left. adj. 1. The distinctive epithet of the hand which is normally the weaker of the two. 2. implying inefficiency of performance." The OED has the following 1650 citation: "Some of our architectors have read some authors about alterations of States with their left eyes which makes them work with their left hands, so sinister."

There is nary a positive connotation to *left*. It is associated with political radicalism. To *be left* is to be abandoned; to be *out in left field* is to be totally off base; and a *left-handed* compliment is unflattering and insincere. The word for "left hand" in Latin, *sinistra*, has given us the highly uncomplimentary *sinister*. The French word for left, *gauche*, in English means "crude and lacking in refinement." Two of the synonyms that *Roget's Thesaurus* lists for "unskillfulness" are *left-handedness* and *gaucherie*.

By contrast, *right* is described in the OED as follows: "Right. adj. 1. straight. . . . 5. disposed to do what is good. . . . 7. correct. . . . 13. sane. . . . 16. legitimate. . . . 18. The distinctive epithet of the hand normally the stronger." Actually, in most languages, as in English, *right* can do no wrong, as the word for right, or a derivative, also means "correct."

Being on the right-hand side means being in a favored position (e.g., "right-hand" man). The word *dextrous* means "highly skilled." It comes from the Latin *dexter*, meaning right. To be *adroit* is to show skill in handling situations. It derives from the French *à droit*, to the right.

In many parts of Africa and Asia, it is still advisable to refrain from using the left hand to eat or to greet. Business cards are best presented with the right hand. In these locales, the left hand is looked at askance by many who feel its use should be restricted to personal hygiene. Such attitudes were not uncommon in the western world before World War II. In a book entitled *Handedness: Right and Left*, published in Boston in 1934, the author Ira S. Wile opines: "Just as pariahs . . . should use only the left hand for contact with impurities, many others would reserve it for use exclusively in the excretory areas. The left hand is the unclean hand; and this incidentally would favor the social usage of the clean and virtuous hand."

Interestingly, the Latin *sinister* originally meant "favorable" as well as "left." It was only later on that it reversed direction and came to mean "unfavorable." What was unfavorable was thus unlucky and to be avoided, lest some misfortune befall the user of the left hand. The word *sinisteritas* was used to designate "awkward behavior."

In France, the definitive word for *left* until the fifteenth century was *senestre*, and then, for unknown etymological reasons, it was supplanted by the word *gauche*. A similar process in Spain predated this. Here the left word, *siniestro*, was replaced by the Basque word for left, *ezker*. Eventually this word transformed into the modern word for left in Spanish, *izquierdo*.

Italian has retained its root word for left, *sinistro*, but it also uses the term *manco* to refer to the left hand. This is derived, as is the French *manqué*, from the Latin *mancus*, which means "maimed and infirm," again based on the concept that the left hand is inferior.

Lefties take heart. Science would seem to imply that left is the preferred direction in both microcosmic and macrocosmic universes. Physicists have discovered that some nuclear particles have a proclivity toward leftward turns. Astronomers have found the same leftward lean. A far greater number of galaxies spin counterclockwise than clockwise. To God, left may indeed be right.

30

Name game is the sport of power players

*I*n a referendum in the 1980s, some Canadians voted "no" to a change in the status quo. I speak, of course, of the good folks of Dildo, Newfoundland, who decided to retain their town's name, notwithstanding its association with a sexual toy.

On the other hand (and other coast), the aboriginal place-names Konshittle Arm and Kowshet Cove were expunged from the map of Vancouver Island in the 1930s. A member of the B.C. Geographical Board justified this bowdlerization thus: "We do not wish to have the daughters of our present and future citizens feel embarrassment in naming the locations of their homes."

And more recently, the Belorussian communities of Zagryazye ("dirty place") and Yazvy ("ulcers") have opted to be known as Bereznyanka ("birch trees") and Vostochnaya ("eastern") respectively. English towns, on the other hand, have not switched. People with surnames such as Piddle, Shitler, and Daft still live in the villages of Ugly, Nasty, Foul Hole, and Swineshead.

Usually, however, a change in the name of a place is an exercise of power. In *Through the Looking Glass* by Lewis Carroll, Alice wonders "whether you can make words mean so many different things." She is corrected by the sagacious egg Humpty Dumpty, who avers "the question is which is the master — that's all."

Globally, the highest proportion of changes to place-names come from the former Soviet Union and China. In *Place Name Changes — 1911–1993*, Adrian Room says, "the broad principle holds that the more turbulent the history of a country, the more numerous are its renamings."

Between 1912, when the last Chinese emperor abdicated, and the establishment of Communist rule in 1949, China endured constant political turmoil. This was reflected in thousands of place-name changes during this period. In the former USSR, it has been estimated that of the total of approximately 700,000 place-names, probably as many as half have undergone changes since the Russian Revolution. In some cases, there have been several changes. Founded in 1703, St. Petersburg became Petrograd in 1914, Leningrad in 1924, and, with the demise of Communism, it has more recently reverted to St. Petersburg. No wonder they call it a revolution.

The African continent has also been active in renaming. Algeria, Angola, and Mozambique have replaced French, Portuguese, and English colonial names, respectively, with indigenous ones. Many countries have themselves been renamed, such as Bechuanaland, Dahomey, Gold Coast, Nyasaland, Rhodesia, and Upper Volta. Not all renamings have been from colonial European names to African names. For example, the former name of Benin, Dahomey, was also an indigenous African name.

Myriad name changes can also be disorienting. Philip Gourevitch, writing in *The Atlantic Monthly*, relates that, in November 1996, a fellow journalist told then rebel leader Laurent Kabila that since Kabila took control of Zaire, bribery was no longer an endemic problem. Kabila responded: "This is not Zaire . . . Zaire is a fabrication of the dictator [Mobutu]. This is the liberated territory of Congo."

Zaire used to be called Congo, but in 1971, in the name of "authenticity," Mobutu conjured up the name Zaire, a Portuguese bastardization of a local word for "river." In the spirit of Louis XIV's *L'état c'est moi*, he was fond of boasting that "there was no Zaire before me, and there will be no Zaire after me." This statement proved to be prophetic, because Kabila's first official act upon becoming president was to restore the name Mobutu had scrapped. And thus was reborn the Democratic Republic of the Congo, capital Kinshasa, which is not to be confused with its neighboring country on the eastern bank of the Congo River, the Republic of the Congo, capital Brazzaville.

Some apparent name changes are really not changes at all. Between 1970 and 1989, Cambodia was called Kampuchea. But Kampuchea is simply a more accurate native spelling of Cambodia. Similarly, the "B" of Burma and the "R" of its capital Rangoon are western approximations of the Burmese sounds that actually begin the names. The place-names Myanmar and Yangon are actually more faithful renderings.

During wars, "enemy" place-names are often eradicated. In World War II, Germany replaced many Polish place-names. For example, Oswiecim was mutated into Auschwitz. In World War I, the South African government supported the British Empire by outlawing all German place-names except Adelaide. As a consequence, Hahndorh became Ambleside, and Lobethal was "ethnically cleansed" into Tweedvale. Similarly, the town of Berlin, Ontario, changed its name to today's Kitchener.

In New Zealand, there was a recent, more frivolous change in the name of a town. In 1986, the prestigious London store Harrods was threatening legal action against some New Zealand businesses bearing the name Harrods. In retaliation, the towns-folk of Otorahanga (pop. 2,500) rechristened their town Harrodsville. One local store in Harrodsville, named (naturally enough) Harrods, sports a window poster that states, "Please visit our London branch when on your next U.K. holiday."

But let us return to Dildo, from where our onomastic journey commenced, to find out whence came the name. The origin of the word is unknown. Its earliest usage was as a refrain in ballads. Canadian place-names maven William Harrison believes that eighteenth-century explorer Captain Cook might have chosen the name for its phallic sense. "Cook . . . had a wicked sense of humor, and it wouldn't be above him to choose a name that might offend some. While the precise origin isn't known, at least it has survived."

Part Five

Commonality: The Bedmates of English

The following chapters focus on languages other than English. Why? I'll let the following quote from a speech by Sir Sridath Ramphal, former secretary-general of the Commonwealth, serve as an explanation: "It is all too easy to make your way in the world linguistically with English as your mother tongue. . . . We become lazy about learning other languages. . . . We all have to make a greater effort. English may be the world's language; but it is not the only language and if we are to be good global neighbors we shall have to be less condescending to the languages of the world — more assiduous in cultivating acquaintances with them."

31

A Frenchman sells bears while an Englishman counts chickens

The Oxford English Dictionary (2nd edition) defines *proverb* as "a short pithy saying in common recognized use . . . which is held to express some truth ascertained by experience or observation and familiar to all."

Though a proverb might be universally understood, often it will be expressed in a way that is peculiar to the society and language in which it originated. Take the Spanish *"En tierra de ciegos, el tuerto es rey"* ("In the land of the blind, the one-eyed man is king"). An equivalent expression exists in French, but not in English or German, so it would appear we have hit upon a peculiarity among speakers of Romance languages. Not so. There is no equivalent expression in Italian, which, like English but unlike Spanish and French, does not possess a noun for "one-eyed man." One has to wonder if the condition of one-eyedness was epidemic at some point in France, because the proverb is pluralized: *"Au royaume des aveugles, les borgnes sont rois."*

The same proverbs can be found in a multitude of languages, but there are almost always significant differences. The English proverb "A bird in the hand is worth two in the bush" in French is not "*Un oiseau dans la main vaut deux dans le buisson*" but "*Un oiseau dans la main vaut deux dans la haie*" ("in the hedge"). This sentiment, however, is more likely to be expressed in French as "*Un tiens vaut mieux que deux tu l'auras*" ("Something you possess is worth more than two things you will have").

In Italian, the equivalent proverb translates as "better a finch in the hand than a thrush on a branch." In German it becomes "Better a sparrow in the hand than a dove on the roof." In Spanish it is "A bird in the hand is worth more than a hundred flying."

English seems to be the only language that takes inventory of chickens, as in "Don't count your chickens before they're hatched." The definitive animal elsewhere seems to be the bear. In French, the maxim states "*Il ne faut pas vendre la peau de l'ours avant de l'avoir tué*" ("Don't sell the bearskin before you've killed the bear"). German, Russian, and Spanish also feature the bear in their equivalent proverbs.

Place-names are likely to change in proverbs and be given a local reference. In England one might "carry coals to Newcastle," whereas in Greece one "sends owls to Athens," and in Spain one transports "iron to Viscaya."

Sometimes a foreign locale can be employed, as in "Rome wasn't built in a day." Like English, German uses Rome, but other languages opt for their own cities, as in "*Paris n'est pas fait en un jour.*" Russian chooses Moscow and Polish eschews its capital Warsaw in favor of Krakow. Spanish also ignores its capital in favor of the rhyming ancient Zamora: "*No se gano Zamora en una hora*" ("Zamora was not won in an hour"). This proverb demonstrates the popularity of rhyme and assonance, as in "Birds of a feather flock together," "When the cat's away, the mice will play," and "A stitch in time saves nine."

For the sake of rhyme, "a stitch" in French saves far more

than nine; it saves one hundred: "*Un point fait à temps en epargne cent.*" Other rhyming French proverbs include "*À bon chat, bon rat*" ("To the good cat, a good rat"); "*Mieux vaut sagesse que richesse*" ("Wisdom is worth more than wealth"); and "*Vouloir, c'est pouvoir*" ("To wish is to be able").

Linguist David Crystal states that many proverbs "can be divided into two parts that balance each other, often displaying parallel syntax and rhythm, and links of rhyme and alliteration." Two examples he lists are the Latin: "*Praemonitus, praemunitus*" ("Forewarned is forearmed"), and the Chinese: "*ai wu ji wu*" ("if you love a house, love its crows").

A proverb is seen by many nowadays as no more than a cliché, for expressing trite, conventional wisdom. In *The Concise Oxford Dictionary of Proverbs*, author John Simpson points out that "in medieval times, and even as late as the 17th century, proverbs often had the status of universal truths and were used to confirm and refute an argument." By the eighteenth century, the esteemed position of proverbs had begun to wane, and those who overused them were mocked. In Samuel Richardson's novel *Clarissa* (1748), a character in a letter writes avuncularly, "It is a long lane that has no turning — Do not despise me for my proverbs."

This is not to say, however, that proverbs have lost their popularity worldwide. The book *Refanero General Ideologoco Espanol* lists 65,000 commonly used Spanish proverbs.

Proverbs probably enjoy their greatest popularity in Africa. Peter Farb, in *Word Play*, states that, outside of the Bushmen of Southern Africa and some speech communities along the Nile, the use of proverbs is pervasive throughout the continent. According to Farb, "proverbs . . . are central to the African judicial process, and litigants quote them to support their cases in much the same way that lawyers in European cultures cite legal precedents to bolster their arguments." They are also used in family disputes, such as those concerning issues of child-rearing, to enhance one's position.

There are some proverbs that seem to contradict each other. For example, the messages of "Look before you leap"/"He who hesitates is lost" and "Nothing ventured, nothing gained"/ "Better safe than sorry" are diametrically opposed to each other.

Here's a challenge: supply the commonly known proverbs whose messages contradict the following:

1) It's never too late to learn.
2) Clothes make the man.
3) If you want something done right, do it yourself.
4) Many hands make light work.
5) Absence makes the heart grow fonder.
6) It's the thought that counts.
7) Wisdom comes with age.
8) Use a carrot instead of a stick.

(*Answers can be found on page 205.*)

32

It's good to swear wild oaths, by Jove

*I*n 1913, a cartoon in the British magazine *Punch* featured an old lady asking a bawling child, "Why are you crying, little boy?" The lad responds, "Because I bean't old enough to swear." And "a good cry, a good laugh, and a good swear," according to Ashley Montagu in *The Anatomy of Swearing*, are all useful means of bringing relief to a troubled mind.

Swear words, according to Montagu, "must have reference to an object possessing, or thought to possess, force or power of some kind." Whereas cursing is a desire for ill fortune to befall one's enemy and is conjugated in the future tense, in swearing one seeks immediate relief, so it is always conjugated in the present tense or the imperative.

While swearing is universal, the means of "sowing wild oaths" varies significantly in different societies. I spoke with Reinhold Aman, editor of *Maledicta, the International Journal of Verbal Aggression*, at his home in Santa Rosa, California. In general, Aman sees a trichotomy of invective at work. African, Asian, and Polynesian insults are familial in nature and include derogatory references to the mother, father, grandparents, or siblings of one's opponent. Protestant societies have a proclivity for swearing that "primarily uses body parts, body functions, sex and excretion." Catholic swearing leans toward "blasphemy, especially the name of the Lord, references to the saints, and references to Church implements."

Gary Bergeron, in "Prayer or Profanity" from *The Anglo's Guide to Survival*, succinctly describes the essence of Québécois swearing: "Know your ecclesiastic terms. Virtually any religious term can be used for swearing, if you say it right. In fact . . . any non-religious term is perfectly clean. For instance, while *sacré tabernacle* would be strong language in front of your shop steward, *c'est tout fucké* is perfectly acceptable in the presence of your mother." Québécois have a penchant for referring to the tabernacle, an ecclesiastical receptacle. This has led to French-Canadians being referred to in Spanish-speaking areas such as the Dominican Republic as "*Los Tabernacos*." Similarly, for a generation after World War I, Americans were known in France as "*sommombiches*."

In Quebec, as in other places that were historically church-dominated, swearing has a cathartic function. In a 1983 *Maledicta* article entitled "Italian Blasphemies," Giuliano Averna states that "for centuries blasphemies [were] the only way of escaping the legal, moral and inquisitorial power of the priest, the confessor and the preacher." Stephen Burgen explains in *Your Mother's Tongue* that religious swearing in Spain reflects an anticlericalism: "When a Catalan says *Em cago en els collons del pare Sant* (I shit on the Pope's balls) it's plain his beef is not with the Almighty but with his earthly representative." Burgen supposes when a Spaniard execrates "I shit on God, on the cross and on the carpenter who made it and on the son of a whore who planted the pine," that "perhaps the speaker had some bad experiences as an altar boy."

Needless to say, it is far more socially acceptable for the excrement you fling to be of a strictly metaphorical nature. *The Anatomy of Swearing* states that "references to excrement and filth doubtless draw their sting for the purposes of swearing from the subjects' obnoxious qualities which, as it were, may be hurled or spattered upon the objects of one's dislike."

Most cultures feature scatological invective, often for emphasis. In Catalan, the most vulgar blasphemies begin with the word *mecagum*, and in the Spanish Gypsy language Gitano with the expression *mecagoen*. Both these terms express a defecatory action.

An Australian aborigine when stubbing his toe is less likely to evoke excrement than to call up the name of a deceased relative. This is not, however, a reflection of his disdain for a departed uncle. Since the names of relatives are considered sacred for a long time after their death, he will take care that the relative has been dead for a long enough period in order to weaken the power of any curse that might be elicited.

Chinese shows a total absence of scatological swearing. This is probably because excrement was a valuable commodity to the peasant as fertilizer. In fact, in olden days, if a peasant was fortunate enough to own a plot of land adjoining a road, he would build an outhouse for the purpose of collecting the valued fertilizing resource.

Nicholas Kristof, writing in *The New York Times Magazine*, claims "there is no language so ill suited to invective as Japanese." There is no Japanese term for the word *jerk*, though there is no more a shortage of jerks in Japan than anywhere else on the planet. Obviously, there is no language academy to advise on proper indigenous usage, because the Japanese must resort to the English word *jerk* to describe one.

The word *kisama* in Japanese is regarded as extremely offensive.

It merely means, however, "your honorable self." Kristof states that "instead of using all kinds of anatomical vocabulary, the Japanese insult each other by frowning and growling 'your honorable self.'"

Comparisons to animals figure prominently in swearing, but there is much variance in the chosen objects of scorn. In most Asian cultures, dogs are viewed negatively as cowardly, unkempt, and prone to stealing. Thus, comparisons to dogs are almost invariably uncomplimentary. In Anglo-Saxon societies, however, a dog is supposedly "man's best friend" and is thus viewed as loyal and clean. Animals such as rats and snakes are used to connote moral turpitude. In France, a camel is associated with very unpleasant characteristics, such as surliness.

A common Hindu curse is to call someone a son of an undesirable animal — perhaps a dog, pig, or bowlegged cow. In Egypt, common insults are the Arabic *ibn ilkalb* or *ibn miza*, "son of a dog" or "son of a goat." In Chinese, a popular insult is the term *wingbadan*, "turtle's egg." The Chinese regard turtles as randy creatures, so the turtle egg reference is a means of questioning paternity and implying incest. Akin is the taunt *tuzaizi*, "baby bunny rabbits," which may be directed at one's enemies to suggest that they copulate like rabbits.

Insulting women is a time-honored universal male ritual. In Chinese, as in most languages, there are far more pejorative terms for women than there are for men. Writing in *Maledicta*, Shumin Huang and D. M. Warren state that in "traditional China women are considered potentially licentious, talkative and untrustworthy."

Even when it comes to insulting women, the Japanese show characteristic temperance. Nicholas Kristof relates that a nasty Japanese expression for a woman is the term *ama*, which means "nun." This is an example of semantic inversion and its intent is sarcastic, implying the opposite of a nun's chastity. But as Kristof points out, "women would probably prefer to be characterized as a nun than as a female dog." In Japanese, as in virtually every language, women are denigrated by terms that question their degree of chastity. Typical among these is the term *baita*, which means "sold woman." Other terms suggest that the proclivity for carnal activity is enjoyed on an amateur as opposed to a professional basis.

Most languages, however, display a paucity of terms for promiscuous men. In traditional China there was no common term for a male virgin. The words for virgin referred strictly to women. Recently, terms like *tong nan*, "child male," have come to fulfil the need to express masculine chastity.

According to Kristof, Japanese women have their own arsenal for insulting men. The most cutting is *maza kon*, derived from the English expression "mother complex." Kristof states that "it means a mama's boy: a wimp who doesn't want to climb Mount Fuji and who doesn't know how to cook rice."

Montagu and others have said that in certain cultures, such as native American and Japanese, swearing hardly exists. Aman, however, disagrees. He believes that swearing is common everywhere, but in some "shamed societies" there is a strong prohibition against public displays of invective.

While swearing may be universal, its severity varies greatly. In an article in *Maledicta*, John Solt wrote that "Japanese maledicta are less direct than those of other countries because subversive language had to be concealed during the time Japan was isolated from the outside world, from 1600 to 1868. Take the expression, *tofu no kado ni atama o butsukete shinde shimae*. While it is a wish for harm to befall your adversary, meaning 'go knock your head on a corner of tofu and die,' its hostility is cushioned by the relative softness of tofu, making death an unlikely occurrence."

Regardless of the degree of invective, swearing serves a valuable purpose. By affording the means of working off the excess energy induced by frustration, the tension level is decreased. Freud said that "the first human being who hurled a curse against his adversary instead of a rock was the founder of civilization." And most probably, at no time do people exhibit fewer inhibitions than when swearing. Looking at different swearing rituals in the world provides us a window by which we discover not only cultural nuances but also a certain similarity of behaviors, which demonstrates the oneness of humanity.

33

Many are trying to get their Irish up

m arch 17 is St. Patrick's Day, the day when the whole world wants to be Irish. It is a joyous occasion, a celebration of life, but for some it is also a reminder of the decline of a proud language.

There are those who find the concept that a seemingly entrenched language can be threatened preposterous at best, and a masquerade for chauvinism at worst. The demise of the Irish language, however, is living proof that a language can vanish.

St. Patrick might have driven the snakes out of Ireland, but it was the English who started the process that drove the Irish language out of its homeland. In the sixteenth century, English settlers assumed positions of importance in Ireland. As a result, the Irish language lost status as the prestige of English was enhanced. In the nineteenth century, famine, and the massive emigration that ensued, gave the English a stronger foothold in

Ireland's political and economic structures, and English became the language necessary for advancement.

A language map of the year 1800 shows only small patches of English spoken in the Dublin area and in Mid-Ulster. By 1851, however, the whole eastern segment of Ireland was English-speaking. Irish Gaelic was spoken as a first language mainly by those who lived on the western seaboard in the area known as the Gaeltacht.

Even with the establishment of an Irish state in 1920, the language has declined further, making it one of the few languages in the world to falter in spite of state protection. In most cases, according to Joshua Fishman in *Reversing Language Shift*, "endangered languages are the receding languages of minority ethnic groups." In the early 1920s there were approximately 250,000 Irish-speakers, but by 1975 the number had fallen to 220,000.

Irish government policy has shifted from one of restoration to one of bilingualism. Both English and Irish are compulsory right through the education system. Opposition to compulsory learning of Irish grew in the 1960s, when some controversial and highly challenged research seemed to indicate that pupils who were educated through the medium of a second language lagged behind in some educational skills. Since the mid-1970s, however, there has been an upsurge in the desire to learn Irish. In North America, "Gaeltacht weekends" were established in 1981 to provide a forum where people interested in the Irish language could congregate and interact as much as possible in that language.

In November 1996, one of these "Irish language weekends" was held at a hotel in the Quebec Laurentians. Participants were asked to "use whatever Irish you have. Try to make sure there is at least one Irish word . . . in each sentence." If people were to use English, they had to "do so with consideration for those of us who don't want to hear it. Go off somewhere where you are out of earshot of others and FEEL GUILTY." Irish, like all the Celtic languages, is difficult to learn because it doesn't sound as it looks and it is highly inflected. An organizer of the conference admitted to me that, although some people do attain a high degree of Irish fluency at the weekend retreats, for most of the attendees it is a way of affirming their identity. Lovers of the Irish language rue that many people of Irish descent eschew learning the Irish language, seeing it as a dead language that conjures up unpleasant memories.

Attempts to increase the first-language use of Irish are not promising. Although two-thirds of the population of Ireland agrees that Irish is crucial for maintaining an Irish identity, half of this two-thirds majority can't speak Irish themselves. Fewer than 2 percent of the people of Ireland use Irish on a regular basis, and even in the Gaeltacht there are only 29,000 users of Irish in daily life. In this Gaelic bastion, many parents choose to educate their children in English "so that they can be like all other Irish children."

The Oxford Companion to the English Language states: "Despite its decline, Irish has a special claim on the Irish. For some, it has symbolic value, like a flag; for others, it is the key to an ancient heritage. It is unlikely, however, that the language will ever again be a vernacular. Such recent trends as a growing demand in urban areas for Irish-medium education, though welcome to those concerned for Gaelic, are unlikely to make a difference."

The short poem "The Death of Irish," by Aidan Carl Mathews, succinctly explains how the Irish language enshrines the essence of the Irish people:

The tide gone out for good,
Thirty-one words for seaweed
Whiten on the foreshore.

34

The glass of language can be replenished

*I*n all probability the peak of language diversity may have occurred before the dawn of civilization. It is calculated that 15,000 years ago there were 10,000 languages serving a population .005 the size of today's population. Languages began dying in droves only from the late fifteenth century onward, when western Europeans started "civilizing" the world. Many aboriginal North American languages are facing extinction within a generation or two, and attempts to revitalize previously entrenched languages have had only limited success.

But language rejuvenators can take heart. Language prognosticators have a spotty track record. Referring to the improbability of being able to revive Hebrew as a vernacular in the twentieth century, the scholar T. Bernfield wrote at the turn of the century: "To make the Hebrew language a spoken tongue in the usual sense of the word is . . . impossible. It has never occurred in any language. . . . A broken glass can no longer be put back together. . . ."

Bernfield was espousing "common knowledge." Writing a decade earlier, the scholar Theodor Noldeke stated: "The dream of some Zionists, that Hebrew will become a living, popular language in Palestine, has still less prospect for realization than their vision of a restored Jewish Empire in the Holy Land." Even Theodore Herzl, the father of Zionism, didn't believe that the vernacularization of Hebrew was really possible in the foreseeable future. Time has proven these men wrong. The broken glass has been pieced together, and from it the Hebrew language flows once again. How did this happen?

With the expulsion of Jews from Israel in A.D. 70, the everyday use of Hebrew faded and was replaced by Aramaic and Greek. Although Hebrew stopped being a vernacular, it retained its position in Jewish communities as a language of study and prayer. Jews in the Diaspora commonly used Ladino, the traditional language of Jews of Spanish descent, or Yiddish for internal communication, and a non-Jewish vernacular for external communication. There were occasions when two Jews from different areas might meet who could communicate only in Hebrew. A Jew from Fez (who didn't speak Yiddish) might meet a Jew from Odessa (who didn't speak Ladino). These encounters, however, were rare.

Hebrew is the only case we know of a language that ceased to be used as a vernacular, and then was subsequently revived. There are several reasons for its renaissance. The Jews of Palestine wanted to break ties to the Diaspora, and a distinct national language was necessary to effectuate this divorce. Also, although English, French, and German were common languages, none of them was dominant enough to stymie Hebrew's resurgence. Hebrew's main rival, Yiddish, never seriously challenged the predominance of Hebrew, for many of the secular Yiddishists were anti-Zionist and didn't immigrate in large numbers.

Eliezer Ben Yehuda, the man most associated with the Hebrew revival, characterized the situation in Palestine as a virtual Babel: "In a small group of twenty persons, ten languages are spoken and no one understands the language of his neighbor." Hebrew was thus able to fill a void by serving as a common vernacular to all the Jewish communities. The Hebrew language was also blessed with many texts with varied Hebraic styles. Other revival attempts, such as those made on behalf of Maori and Irish Gaelic, have been hampered by a lack of widespread knowledge of the written language.

Hebrew's revival has been characterized as a "miracle." It was not. The scholar Cohn-Schacter wrote, "Hebrew had lost only the language of the market and the kitchen. Hebrew was on the threshold of speech." Joshua Fishman describes Hebrew's revival as "the rare and largely fortuitous co-occurrence of language-and-nationality ideology, disciplined collective will and sufficient societal dislocation from other competing influences to make possible a rapid and clean break with prior norms of verbal interaction. . . ."

According to linguist Kenneth L. Hale, no case is hopeless. "Take Mohican, there aren't any speakers . . . but you could take books and deeds published back in the 1600s, and from what we know about comparative Algonquin, you could figure out pretty closely what it sounded like. People could learn it and begin to use it and revive it."

The Israeli writer Naftali Tur-Sinai states that "even an artificial language which has never been alive, such as Esperanto, can be made to live, if only there is a recognized need for it and a stubborn will of people to make it come alive."

35

Just because someone's deaf doesn't mean she can't hear

*A*t a recent graduation ceremony at the Lexington Center
for the Deaf in New York City, a speaker stated that "from the
time God made earth until today, this is probably the best time
to be deaf." Much of this upbeat attitude has to do with the
greater acceptance of sign language as a "real" language. It has,
however, been an arduous struggle.

The use of sign language was actually banned by "experts" in
the education of the deaf at the Congress of Milan in 1880, and
this negative attitude pervaded the first half of this century.
Deafness was seen by most psychologists and educators of the
deaf as a form of pathology. Deaf people were seen as "sick,"
and the cure was teaching them to read lips and to produce artificial speech that speech therapists deemed intelligible.

Even quite recently the idea has persisted that only spoken
language is truly a language. John Lyons, in his 1981 textbook
Language and Linguistics, affirms that "sign language . . . or the

language of the bees would be considered by most people as a metaphorical use of language." For Lyons, true language depends on sound, and he thus dismissed what he called "the language of the deaf and dumb."

In 1815, the Reverend Thomas Gallaudet of Connecticut traveled to Paris and visited the only institute in the world that educated the deaf by using sign language. He persuaded Laurent Clerc, a teacher at the institute, to return with him to America to establish a similar school in Hartford. The French sign language was wed to indigenous American signs and a dialect used on Martha's Vineyard (where there was a high incidence of hereditary deafness) to form American Sign Language (ASL). Today ASL is used by approximately 500,000 deaf people in Canada and the United States. This makes it the fourth largest "first" language in the United States.

In 1968, neuroscientist Ursula Bellugi designed an experiment that compared how "normal" children with hearing learn to speak versus the manner in which deaf children communicate by using sign language. Her interest lay not in studying sign language as such, but in extrapolating differences between hearing and deaf children as a means of discovering how language is processed in the brain. Language at the time was thought to depend on the ability to speak. Sign language was seen as a primitive type of communication, akin to a pidgin at best. When Bellugi began her research she knew nothing about sign language, but then again, neither did the experts. Some linguists said it was a collection of pictorial gestures; others that it was essentially derived from spoken language. It seemed to her that the theories rested more on folklore than science.

One person's concept, however, intrigued her. William Stokoe was a teacher at Gallaudet University in Washington, D.C., the world's only liberal arts university for the deaf. Stokoe's experience working with the deaf made him realize that signing was more than just crude gesturing. He deduced that signs were comprised of distinct components — the shapes one made with one's hands, where the hands were placed, and how the hands were moved. This reminded him of the distinct component in the sound system of spoken language, the phoneme. For Bellugi, the essence of a language is its grammar, and in studies of ASL she discovered that grammar for signers depends on space, hand shapes, and movements as opposed to sound sequences. In her 1979 book *The Signs of Language*, she concluded that sign *is* language.

Peter Radetsky, in an August 1994 article in *Discover* magazine, gave the following explanation of the mechanics of sign language: "In ASL, to say 'The girl looks at the boy,' a signer places the sign for 'girl' at one point in space, and the sign for 'boy' at another, then moves the "look" sign from one point toward the other. . . . To say 'The girl is looking at the boy,' the look sign is modified by a . . . change in hand movement; the continuous action of looking is conveyed by moving the hand like a Ferris wheel from the girl toward the boy and back full circle to the girl again. What's more, the face is a fund of grammatical information. Very particular facial movements (a certain way of raising and lowering the eyebrows, of pursing and clenching the lips) fill in information about relative clauses, questions and adverbial nuances."

Bellugi says that in signing "it's as if there's a stage. There's a very distinct plane in space, right here [the area from waist level to face, and from shoulder to shoulder], where the action is taking place." You, the listener, are like a front-row spectator at a play watching a drama unfold. Don't blink, or you'll miss part of the performance, because fluent signing entails one or two signs per second.

The similarities of sign to speech are remarkable. In work pioneered by cognitive psychologist Laura Petito, it was discovered that deaf infants whose parents sign to them will "babble" with their hands at the same stage that hearing babies whose parents coo to them babble. Also, the same critical period for language acquisition applies in sign as in speech — between eighteen and thirty-six months — and diminishes greatly in both spheres after the age of twelve years.

Just as people who speak have words on the "tip of their tongues," signers have signs on the "tip of their fingers."

As long as one has a mind, one can hear.

Part Six

Jollity: The Play of English

Tony Augarde, in his introduction to *The Oxford Guide to Word Games*, says that "one of the most lovable characteristics of human beings is their persistent tendency to find new and frivolous use of things. Words were designed for the serious business of communicating but humans constantly devise novel uses for them."

Put another way, the re-creation of language is recreation. The English language, with its huge vocabulary of heteronyms, allows for much fun with words.

In this closing segment, I'll explore some of these playful avenues.

36

Riddles can be fun and games, or life and death

> *Question*: What do you call a boomerang
> that won't come back?
> *Answer*: A stick.

> *Question*: Why did the tomato turn red?
> *Answer*: He saw the salad dressing.

*T*hese conundrums were posed to yours truly by my seven-year-old niece Katie. Alas, she found her Uncle Homer wanting. She was grilling me from a book called *Kids Are Funny: Jokes Sent by Kids to the Rosie O'Donnell Show.*

Some of the riddles in this collection have been around at least since I was seven. Standing the test of time are such old favorites as "Question: What has four wheels and flies? Answer: A garbage truck"; and "Question: Why did the girl throw the butter out the window? Answer: She wanted to see butter fly." Some riddles, however, have been updated: "Question: Why did the bubble gum cross the road? Answer: Because it was stuck to the chicken's leg." Technological advances allow other riddles, such as "Question: What type of mouse won't eat cheese? Answer: A computer mouse."

Iona and Peter Opie compiled riddles from British children in the 1950s. In their book *The Lore and Language of*

Schoolchildren, they relate that many of the riddles submitted were two centuries old. In fact the riddle "Question: How deep is the ocean? Answer: A stone's throw" and the riddle "Question: How many balls of string would it take to reach the moon? Answer: One, if it was long enough" can be found in *Demaundes Joyous*, a book of riddles printed in 1511 in London.

Peter Farb, in *Word Play*, relates that "the majority of children are strikingly punctual in acquiring a repertory of riddles at about six or seven, and at that age they will tell about three times as many joking riddles as jokes in any other form. During the next several years, riddles continue to make up about a half of a child's store of jokes, and it is not until about the age of eleven that they are discarded in favor of anecdotes."

Ancient riddles were hardly child's play, and virtually all civilizations feature riddling contests among adults. Rather than being phrased as a question, these riddles were usually delivered as enigmatic statements. For example, in the Book of Judges, Samson offers this conundrum: "Out of the eater came something to eat; out of the strong came something sweet." Delilah uses her charms to worm the answer from him: that he had seen a swarm of bees making honey in the carcass of a lion. Later in the Bible, it is related in 1 Kings "that when the queen of Sheba heard of the fame of Solomon, she came to prove him with hard questions. And Solomon told her all her questions: there was not any thing hid from the king."

In many ancient riddle contests, the penalty for losing the contest was the forfeiture of one's life. J. R. R. Tolkien, in *The Hobbit*, highlights this tradition in the chapter entitled "Riddles in the Dark, where Gollum and Bilbo try to guess each other's riddles in a life and death battle of wits." Of course, Sophocles painted this scenario much earlier. Oedipus, while on his way to Thebes, encounters the Sphinx and stakes his life on solving its riddle: "What walks on four legs in the morning, two legs at noon, and three legs in the evening?" The answer is man, who crawls as an infant, walks upright as an adult, and uses a staff in old age. Oedipus thus destroys the Sphinx and is proclaimed the King of Thebes. Along with the throne, he is rewarded with the royal widow Jocasta, who turns out to be his mother. This eventually destroys Oedipus but delights psychiatrists two millennia later.

Riddles also played an important role in ancient life-cycle rituals, such as weddings and funerals. J. G. Frazer relates in *The Golden Bough* that "in Brittany, after a burial, when the rest have gone to partake of the funeral banquet, old men remain behind in the graveyard and ask each other riddles."

Perhaps in our culture, riddling has been relegated to the domain of inquisitive seven-year-olds like my niece Katie, intent on tormenting their uncles. Nevertheless, they provide a valuable service. According to Farb, "instead of offering children specific instructions for day-to-day living, riddles are a more subtle education for life in general. They are steppingstones to adulthood because they prepare the child for an important aspect of life in all cultures. Apparently the riddle affords excellent preparation for the role which speakers will assume as adults in their speech communities."

Riddles may no longer play the ceremonial role described in Frazer's *The Golden Bough*. By reveling in riddles, children are helping keep alive a part of our heritage that otherwise might be lost. Keep it up, Katie!

37

The many varieties of Scrabble

*I*t was 1931, the height of the Great Depression, when American architect Alfred Butts joined the bulging ranks of the unemployed. There just weren't many buildings being built, so Butts decided to construct something else — an adult game.

He called his game Lexico. It was played without a board, and players received points based on the lengths of the words formed. One would receive bonus points for using less-common letters such as F and W, and very rare letters like Q and Z would fetch you an even higher score.

How did Butts do his letter-value computing in the pre-cyber era? He meticulously checked the frequency of letters on the front pages of *The New York Times*. He came up with a formula that employed 100 tiles including 12 Es, 9 each of the second most common letters, A and I, and the rest of the alphabet in decreasing frequency, with only 1 tile each for Z, X, Q, K, and J.

In 1938, the popularity of crossword puzzles gave Butts the

idea of combining the letters with a playing board in which words could be joined. In this newer version, Butts's game was marketed under several other names. They included New Anagrams, Alph, Criss-Cross, Criss Crosswords, and finally the one that stuck, in 1948: Scrabble.

Since the mid-1950s, Scrabble has enjoyed a meteoric rise, and for many years it has had two official lexicons dedicated to it. They are the *Official Scrabble Players Dictionary* (OSPD), published by Merriam-Webster, and *Official Scrabble Words* (OSW), published by Chambers Dictionary. Generally speaking, the former is used in North America and the latter is used in Great Britain. In some competitions, words are accepted when found in either lexicon. This list is informally called SOWPODS, a marriage of the seven letters in OSPD and OSW.

One will find many curious two-lettered and three-lettered English words in these sources that are not found in most dictionaries. Some examples are *aa*, *ba*, and *ghi*, which refer respectively to "rough cindery lava," "eternal soul" (Egyptian), and "a type of butter." Since October 1995, however, the OSPD has shunned some politically incorrect words. Nowhere in the ESPD, *Expurgated Scrabble Players Dictionary*, will you find such potentially hurtful words as *fatso*, *faggotry*, *whities*, and *shiksa*.

Over 100 million Scrabble games have been sold in over 120 countries. Speakers of over thirty different languages can now play in their distinct tongues, with values and letter frequencies based on each particular language.

While waiting on the phone at the largely French-speaking company where I recently worked, I perused a list of the sixty-two names of my fellow office employees. In an epiphanous moment worthy of Archimedes, it dawned on me that I was in possession of something unique — the letter W in my name. This dearth of the letter W in French is rewarded by its letter value in the French version of Scrabble rising from a mere four points to an enviable ten.

Others too have mused on the different letter frequencies in other tongues and how it impinges on Scrabble. In an article in *The Observer* several years ago, Jennifer Frankel wrote of enjoying a meal in a Polish restaurant, which consisted of *barszcz* (beetroot soup) and *kaczka* with *kasza* (roast duck with cracked wheat). She opined, "With words full of Zs like that, it must be very odd playing Scrabble in Poland. . . . Make the word barszcz" in English, she adds, "and you're 29 up, even before adding any triple-letter or triple-word scores or the fifty bonus for using all seven letters. There's a problem, though. There's only one Z in the English version."

In Polish, a Z is worth only one point, not ten as in English. Because of the frequency of Polish Zs, there are five of them in the Polish game, and *barszcz* yields the player only ten points. The Polish version, like the English one, consists of 100 tiles, but 32 of these are different letters, including three one-point Zs and two more valuable accented ones. Scrabble in other languages is also highly distinctive. The 32 different letters available to Polish Scrabble players seem paltry compared to the 38 available in Hungarian, and that is without Q, W, X, and Y. German Scrabble until recently had not only more letters than English, 117, but also more tiles for each move. Instead of the standard seven tiles, German players received eight. In English, the consonant-to-vowel ratio is 60:40, whereas in Italian the ratio is 50:50 and there are 20 percent more tiles. Not surprisingly, Italian Scrabble features 15 Os.

For those who revel in statistics, I collected the following data from a Scrabble website. The highest score ever attained in a Scrabble game was 1,049 by Brit Phil Appleby in 1989. The highest word score for a single play is 392 for the word *caziques*. It was first achieved in 1982 in Manchester, England.

Alas, humanity has suffered another stinging defeat to a computer. First, Deep Blue vanquished chess champion Garri Kasparov. Recently, to mark Scrabble's fiftieth anniversary, a tournament was held. The contestants were two Scrabble masters, Matt Graham and Joel Sherman, versus the computer program Maven, created by Brian Shepherd. The final score, in games, was Maven 6, Graham-Sherman 3.

38

There's more than one way to go from black to white in wordplay

*I*n 1879, Lewis Carroll introduced a form of linguistic alchemy to the pages of *Vanity Fair* magazine. In a game he dubbed Doublets, a word is changed letter by letter, always forming another word, until the second given word is reached. Carroll explained that the word *head* can become the word *tail* by interposing the words *heal, teal, tell,* and *tall.* Ever a proper Victorian, he added, "needless to state it is de rigueur that the links should be English words, such as might be used in good society."

Perhaps influenced by his contemporary Darwin, Carroll evolved *ape* into *man* in this six-step method: *ape-are-ere-err-ear-mar-man.* This evolutionary process can be shortened, however, by this sequence: *ape-apt-opt-oat-mat-man.* Here are some other word transpositions.

WHEAT to BREAD: *wheat-cheat-cheap-cheep-creep-creed-breed-bread*

ONE to TWO: *one-owe-ewe-eye-dye-doe-toe-too-two*

FOUR to FIVE: *four-foul-fool-foot-fort-fore-fire-five*

BLACK to WHITE: *black-slack-stack-stalk-stale-shale-whale-while-white*

Prior to the nineteenth century, English word puzzles were mostly restricted to riddles and enigmas, with the goal being not so much to puzzle the reader as to entertain him. In the early 1800s, however, two puzzle anthologies, entitled *The Masquerade* and *A New Collection of Enigmas*, were published in England, and they featured puzzles based on word patterns, such as "beheaded" words (*stone-tone-one*) and "curtailed" words (*rabbit-rabbi*).

Will Shortz relates two of these nineteenth-century puzzles. *A New Collection of Enigmas* featured this 1806 "beheaded" puzzle.

Tho' small I am, yet, when entire,
I've force to set the world on fire.
Take off a letter, and 'tis clear
My paunch will hold a herd of deer:
Dismiss another, and you'll find
I once contain'd all human kind.

(The answer is *spark-park-ark*.)

One of the famous early nineteenth-century word puzzles is the following "curtailed" word penned by future prime minister of England (albeit for only four months) George Canning.

A word there is of plural number,
Foe to ease and tranquil slumber;

Any other word you take
And add an s will plural make.
But if you add an s to this,

So strange the metamorphosis;
Plural is plural now no more,
And sweet what bitter was before.

(The answer is *cares-caress.*)

Shortz admits that many of the puzzles in popular publications were of poor quality and nothing more than childish diversions. The best of the puzzles, however, he describes as "an art through which many of the leading intellectuals of the times entertained themselves."

Since at least the time of the ancient Greeks, all civilizations have practiced wordplay. Unlike recreational mathematics, however, wordplay was not until quite recently perceived to be worthy of study. This changed in 1965 with Dmitri Borgmann's *Language on Vacation*. Borgmann resurrected an ancient word, *logology*, to describe the study of words not for linguistic purposes but for their recreational value.

The essence of logology is discovering word patterns. Some examples are palindromes, words spelled the same backwards as forwards ("deified"); tautonyms, words with a repeated syllable ("murmur"); words in which the letters fall in alphabetical order ("almost"); and long words, called isograms, in which no letters repeat themselves ("ambidextrously").

Also part of the logological quest is to show how words can be transformed into other words. The word *sheathed* can be reduced to the word *a* by successively dropping letters: *sheathed-sheathe-sheath-heath-heat-eat-at-a*. And *stop* can become *go* by selective deletions and insertions of letters: *stop-top-to-tot-tout-out-gout-got-go*.

In a 1967 book, *Beyond Language*, Borgmann performed a semantic version of Carroll's Doublets by employing synonyms. *Black* becomes *white* and *ugly* turns *beautiful* in the following manners: BLACK-*dark-obscure-hidden-concealed-snug-comfortable-easy-simple-pure*-WHITE; UGLY-*offensive-insulting-insolent-proud-lordly-stately-grand-gorgeous*-BEAUTIFUL.

Playing with words, I believe, is part of the literary process. Devices such as rhyme and alliteration are essentially means of finding word patterns. Thinking under the constraints of word-play can act as a form of linguistic medicine ball for those of us who have allowed our literary muscles to get flabby.

39

The anagram — ah, an art gem

Is pity love? Positively!
Desperation. A rope ends it.

*D*on't worry, logophiles. I am not dispensing advice for the loveless and hopeless. *Positively* is an anagram of *Is pity love?* and *A rope ends it* is an anagram of *desperation*. An anagram is a word or phrase made by rearranging the letters of another word or phrase. As in the above examples, a good anagram should reflect the meaning of the base word or phrase.

The term *anagram* is sometimes used to refer to any word that can be rearranged to form a new word (*triangle* can be turned into *integral*, and *agnostic* can be transformed into *coasting*). Technically, these are examples of transposals and not of anagrams.

In 1903, in his *Handy-Book of Literary Curiosities*, English writer William Walsh lamented that "so few really good anagrams have been rolled down to us. . . . All the really superb anagrams . . . might be contained in a pillbox." The last century's inclusions might have necessitated a breadbox instead of a pillbox, but there is still a dearth of great anagrams.

O. V. Michaelsen, in an article published in the journal *Word Ways* in 1990, lays down the criteria for a top-notch anagram.

1) It must be self-explanatory. For example, the anagram:

That's prime news? No, it preys on the week
The newspaper is not the New York Times

is deficient because it must be explained that it refers to a newspaper which regards sensationalism as real news.

2) It must not contain unnecessary words:

The great Thomas Alva Edison
The good man, he lit vast areas

Here, the unnecessary words *the great* detract from the theme. Interjectory words such as *oh*, *eh*, and *ah* should also be avoided.

3) There should never be more than three letters appearing in the same sequence they assumed in the original word(s).

4) An anagram should either complete a sentence or be complete in itself. Michaelsen says the anagram to *A trip around the world, Hard to plan wider tour*, is not complete because, grammatically, it should read, "a wider tour."

Based on these criteria, here are ten apt anagrams.

1) *eleven + two = twelve + one*
2) *the nudist colony : no untidy clothes*
3) *endearment : tender name*
4) *a shoplifter : has to pilfer*

5) *the eyes : they see*
6) *an aisle : is a lane*
7) *animosity : is no amity*
8) *Salman Rushdie : dare shun Islam*
9) *a sentence of death : faces one at the end*
10) *editorials : adroit lies*

Closely associated with *anagrams*, which "reflect" the original meaning, are *antigrams*, which "deflect" the original sense. Here are ten examples of this contradictory genre.

1) *forty-five : over fifty*
2) *antagonist : not against*
3) *diplomacy : mad policy*
4) *funeral : real fun*
5) *violence : nice love*
6) *protectionism : nice to imports*
7) *Santa : Satan*
8) *adversaries : are advisers*
9) *enormity : more tiny*
10) *militarism : I limit arms*

Considering that anagrams are seen as a form of revealed truth, it is not surprising that anagrams with a religious theme have been popular. The Latin version of Pilate's question to Jesus, "*Quid est veritas?*" ("What is truth?") has been rendered anagrammatically as "*Est vir qui adest*" ("It is the man who is before you"). *Christian* has been turned into *rich saint* and *rich at sin*. *Christianity* has become *I cry that I sin* and *It's in charity*. *Evangelist* has been mutated into *evil's agent*; and *Presbyterians* have been described as *best in prayers*.

It would appear that soon we will need a larger box to contain our anagrammatic treasures. Our newest jewels, however, will probably be cyber-crafted and not handcrafted. In 1994,

Ross Eckler, the editor of *Word Ways,* gave a "hand" anagrammist and computer-aided anagrammist the challenge of creating an anagram for the expression *The center cannot hold.* The unassisted human mind came up with a dozen renditions, with the best offering being *Or let the hand connect.* The computer rendered 300,000 anagrams, the best being *He can't control the end.*

Though transposals appear to present less of a challenge to wordplay enthusiasts, they can become more difficult if they are restricted to a specific category. For example, the words *animal, avenge, diagnose, hasten, Havanans, nominates, oration,* and *salvages* can be scrambled to produce the following place-names: *Manila, Geneva, San Diego, Athens, Savannah, Minnesota, Ontario,* and *Las Vegas.*

In the following list, can you guess what nationalities have been ethnically mutated through transposals? *Cinerama, saturnalia, Lachine, raincoat, shingle, himself, manger,* and *valiant.* Respectively, the answers are *American, Australian, Chilean, Croatian, English, Flemish, German,* and *Latvian.*

Similarly, *Argentines, aridness, assuage, solemn,* and *throbs* all become edible words when transmogrified respectively into *tangerines, sardines, sausage, melons* or *lemons,* and *broths.*

The most interesting transposals are of long words in which the resultant pairs have very different patterns of letters. Some examples here are *allegorist : legislator; enumeration : mountaineer;* and *partitioned : trepidation.*

Many words can be transposed into another word — such as *march* into *charm* — but not that many can be transposed more than once. Readers are thus asked to complete each sentence by filling in the blanks with three words that are anagrams of each other. For example, to complete the sentence: "Since their friendship was so _____ to her, Anne didn't _____ _____ her roommate's diary," you would add the words *dear, dare,* and *read.* The missing words get longer as you go along.

1) Between _____ of Webber's _____, the whiskered _____ waited backstage.

2) The photo showed a man in faded _____ and the headline read: "_____ _____ and is working at a car wash."

3) At the _____ trial, the prosecutor alleged that the woman danced with the Devil and convinced ten _____ to nosh in between _____.

4) When Bill Bennett was _____ leader he _____ many victories notwithstanding his whacko _____.

5) His winning _____ as a _____ was such that when he challenged racers of 500 through 5000 meters to beat him, there were no _____.

6) Lucien Bouchard doesn't _____ having assumed the _____ of leadership even though it has proved to be a _____ strain.

7) The day the hippie _____ his cool _____ was the _____ day of his life.

8) Only _____ goalies aren't injured by net crashers, so _____ penalties will be needed to _____ this trend.

9) The chief _____ examiner _____ that a _____ point had been shifted in the hospital's financial report.

10) Canadian _____ lamented that the _____ athlete had used an illicit _____.

11) If Paul Martin _____ the national debt, he'll have _____ the Canadian economy and _____ his place in history as a great finance minister.

12) The President's claim that it was an _____ illusion that he had groped the intern was a _____ issue on _____ Hill.

13) Though her husband constantly _____ her, Helen _____ to a real change in her life and not merely changing _____.

14) During his _____ classes at the hospital, John learned that his upcoming duties would be both _____ and _____.

15) _____ people to the dangers of STDs is _____ in _____ their behavior.

16) Even the _____ _____ were unable to hide the _____ guerrilla from his pursuers.

17) The _____ _____ out of the Ukraine couldn't envisage that one day their children would not only be speaking but _____ the English language.

18) Although _____ by his parents, Steve _____ his college _____ by binge drinking.

19) The movie critic's view that Andy Griffith's role in *No Time for* _____ establishes his_____ as an actor _____ him from most of his peers.

(*Answers can be found on pages 205–6.*)

40

Mary had a little lipogram, and the fox waltzed in the pangram

*A*nagrams and isograms are not the only "gram" wordplay stars. Here is another:

Lipogram: This is defined by *Webster's Third International Dictionary* as "a writing not having a certain letter," but such a definition is not satisfactory. In short passages it is not uncommon for some of the less common letters of the alphabet — such as "x" or "z" — not to appear. By common convention, the letter or letters that do not appear are supposed to be common letters for the passage to be considered a lipogram.

Lipograms represent one of the most ancient forms of wordplay. Joseph Addison related in *The Spectator* in 1711 that the fifth-century Greek poet Tryphiodorus "composed an Odyssey or epic poem of the adventures of Ulysses," consisting of twenty-four books. In each of the books, Tryphiodorus avoided the use of a different letter of the alphabet in order to prove, according to Addison, "that he could do his business without them."

This lipogrammatic tradition continued in Rome and Persia and regained popularity in Europe in the seventeenth century, particularly in Spain. In 1939, Ernest Vincent Wright wrote a 50,000-word novel without ever using the most common letter, "e." The Frenchman Georges Perec also avoided the use of an "e" in his 1969 novel *La Disparition*.

Ross Eckler, editor of *Word Ways*, has rendered Sara Josepha Hale's classic "Mary Had a Little Lamb" in five lipogrammatic variations, omitting its most common letters: "s," "h," "t," "e," and "a." Here are the "e" and "s" elisions:

Mary had a tiny lamb,
Its wool was pallid as snow,
And any spot that Mary did walk
This lamb would always go;
This lamb did follow Mary to school,
Although against a law;
How girls and boys did laugh and play,
That lamb in class all saw.

Mary had a little lamb,
With fleece a pale white hue,
And everywhere that Mary went
The lamb kept her in view;
To academe he went with her,
Illegal, and quite rare:
It made the children laugh and play
To view a lamb in there.

Skeptical readers might be wondering how Eckler rendered "Mary" in his "a" elision. "Mary" became "Polly" and the "lamb" turned into a "sheep."

Not to be outdone, Gyles Brandeth, in *The Joy of Lex*, renders Hamlet's famed soliloquy without an "i."

To be, or not to be; that's the query:
Whether you would be nobler to suffer mentally
The stones and arrows of outrageous fortune,
Or to take arms oppose a sea of troubles,
And through combat end them? To pass on, to sleep;
No more . . .

Imposing lipogrammatic constraints is probably good training for creative writing because it compels the writer to select words very carefully and to express ideas in an original manner. It can also demonstrate that, even when one is unable to employ many words, not only can the writing be sensible, it can remain strong.

Now, take the following sentence: *The quick brown fox jumps over the lazy dog.* When learning how to type you might have tapped out this improbable sentence. This type of sentence is called a *pangram* because it uses all 26 letters of the alphabet in a relatively short space (here, in 35 letters).

Don't be fooled by the brevity of our fox-dog sentence into believing that the average paragraph will contain all the letters of the alphabet. In fact, it has been calculated that in a passage of two thousand words there is only a 50 percent probability that all the letters of the alphabet will be used. There are two reasons for this. First, there are only five main vowels in the alphabet, and this means that the letters "a," "e," "i," "o," and "u" appear a disproportionate amount of the time. Also, the consonants "j," "q," "x," and "z" are relatively rare. The letter "x" occurs every 625th letter, "q" and "j" every thousandth letter, and the caboose of the alphabet, "z," every 1,700th letter.

In *The Oxford Guide to Word Games*, author Tony Augarde quotes writer Alastair Reid who says: "[T]he dream which preoccupies the tortuous mind of every palindromist is that somewhere within the confines of the language lurks the Great Palindrome . . . flowing sweetly in both directions, but which also contains the Final Truth of Things." In the same manner, the quest for the perfect pangram has obsessed many wordsmiths. Sensewise, however, pangrams are the antithesis to palindromes. For in palindromes the sense increases with the brevity of the palindromic statement; in pangrams sense usually deteriorates proportionately with brevity.

The ideal pangram employs each letter only once, but composing intelligible sentences in this manner is problematic. They often feature dubious words not found in many dictionaries, such as *cwm*, a word of Welsh derivation meaning "valley." Take the following 26-letter "perfect" pangram: *Vext cwm fly zing jabs Kurd qoph.* It translates into discernible English as "an annoyed fly in a valley, humming shrilly, pokes at the nineteenth letter of the Hebrew alphabet drawn by a Kurd." *The Oxford Companion to the English Language* cites two pangrams that contain no more than 26 letters. The first one is the rather enigmatic *Quiz my black-Whigs-export fund.* The second pangram is only slightly more intelligible — *Blowzy night-frumps vex'd Jack Q.* — but it "cheats" by using two abbreviations. Another pangrammatic loophole is to use initialed individuals, as in *J. Q. Schwartz flung D. V. Pike my box.*

Even almost perfectly brief pangrams are apt to feature peculiar themes. In only 29 letters, we are told that *Foxy nymphs grab quick-lived waltz.* One letter shorter is the pangram *Waltz nymph, for quick jigs vex Bud.* Greater variation emerges as we allow over 30 letters to appear in our pangrams, as in *Jackdaws love my big sphinx of quartz* (31 letters) and *Pack my box with five dozen liquor jugs* (32 letters).

People have gone to great lengths searching for pangrams in literary works. There are over 27,000 verses in the King James Version of the Bible, yet nary a one is a perfect pangram. The closest the Bible comes to pangrammatic fulfillment is the following 172-lettered passage from Ezra 7:21: "*And I, even I Artaxerxes the king, do make a decree to all the treasurers which are beyond the river, that whatsoever Ezra the priest, the scribe of the law of the God of heaven, shall require of you, it be done speedily."*

Alas, there is a letter of the alphabet missing from this verse, the letter "j." The next closest biblical passage can be found in 1 Chronicles 12:40. It uses 216 letters but not one of them is a "q."

Wordsmith Howard Bergerson searched all of Shakespeare's 154 sonnets in a quest for the pangrammatic Holy Grail. His forbearance was rewarded only once, in Sonnet 27, which uses all the letters of the alphabet in a mere 451 letters.

English-language word alchemists are not alone in their quest for pangrams. According to OULIPO's* *Atlas de Littérature*, perhaps the shortest French pangram is *Whisky vert: jugez cinq fox d'aplomb* (29 letters). *Whisky* seems to be featured in French pangrams, probably because of the dearth of "ws." Two other French pangrams are *Zoe, grande fille, veut que je boive ce whisky, mais je veux pas* and *Portez ce vieux whisky au juge blond qui fume.*

While surfing the Internet, I discovered Dutch and German pangrams. The former is *Zweedse ex-VIP behoorlijk gekop quantum fysica* ("Swedish ex-VIP pretty crazy about quantum physics") and the German *Zwei Boxka mpfer jagen Eva quer durch Sylt* ("Two boxers hunt Eva every which way through Sylt").

Lipograms and pangrams are probably best appreciated as participatory endeavors. Out there lurks a 26-letter pangram possessing exquisite sense and beauty. And somewhere the greatest novel since *Ulysses* is waiting, but this time written without the benefit of the letter "s." So get your pencils out and commence your "grammatic" masterpieces.

---

* OULIPO, or *Ouvroir de Littérature Potentielle*, is a group of twenty mathematicians and writers who meet once a month in Paris to discuss potential literary forms.

41

Coming or going, palindromes have much to say

Able was I ere I saw Elba.
Madam, I'm Adam.

*T*he above are two of the best-known *palindromes* in the English language. For those of you who weren't paying attention in English class, a quick refresher: a palindrome is a word, sentence, or phrase that reads the same backwards and forwards.

In the face of seemingly insurmountable odds, palindromic statements not only form words but also make sense when reversed. The use of palindromes has been common in many languages and cultures. The ancient Greeks often put the palindrome *nispon anomimata mi monan opsin* on fountains. It means "Cleanse your sins as well as the face." The Romans also fancied palindromes, demonstrated by *In girum imus nocte et consumimur igni*, which translates as "We enter the circle after dark and are consumed by fire." Another palindromic form used by the Romans was the word-square, where the message could be read both vertically and horizontally:

ROTAS
OPERA
TENET
AREPO
SATOR

This translates as "Arepo, the sower, guides the wheels at work," which is a way of saying that God controls the universe. The symmetry of a palindrome holds a magical attraction for the human mind because of the order it creates. In a sense it is the West's equivalent to the Chinese concept of *yin* and *yang*, which postulates that the interaction between opposing forces creates a symmetry in the universe.

The balance required in constructing palindromes appears at first glance to be daunting. The English language poses some added problems because of the consonantal arrangement in some frequently used words, such as *the* and *and*. In fact, it has been calculated that the likelihood of a palindrome of eighteen letters occurring naturally in written English is one million to one. This means that even small, mediocre palindromes are improbable. Those that express an intelligible thought are virtually miraculous.

But fear not, inventing palindromes is not as difficult as it first appears.

Take the palindrome at the top of page 189, *Able was I ere I saw Elba*, referring to the exiled Napoleon. Let's analyze the structure. The middle segment, *I ere I*, reads the same in both directions. Since *was* backwards reads *saw*, the balance is still maintained when we include these words, *was I ere I saw*. The symmetry then persists when we add the word pair *able* and *Elba*.

Because the statement is palindromic without the first and last words, any word pairs that replace these words will keep the palindrome in order. Two word pairs that maintain balance while making sense are *snug-guns* and *stressed-desserts*. They provide us with *Snug was I ere I saw guns* and *Stressed was I ere I saw desserts*. Getting a bit more devious (and a lot more raunchy), we can use the words *a slut* to balance *Tulsa*. This yields us *A slut was I ere I saw Tulsa*.

In *Madam, I'm Adam* there is also a core palindrome within the palindromic sentence. The core segment is *m I'm*, which is comprised of the last letter in *Madam* and the word *I'm*. Therefore, to create a new palindrome keeping the *m I'm* part intact, we must find balanced parts on both sides. Three possibilities that fulfil this criterion are: *Norm, I'm Ron, Adam, I'm Ada*, and *Warm? I'm raw!*

Ironically, many words that have a religious connotation work well in word pairs. Some examples are *evil-live, devil-lived,* and *God-dog.* The word *deified* is itself a palindrome, as is the name *Eve.* Even *Adam* works palindromically in the *Madam-Adam* pairing.

The challenge in composing palindromes is in striking a balance between length and meaning. There is an inverse ratio between a palindrome's size and its sense. As the equation becomes longer, it becomes more likely that logic will be sacrificed.

Names can be very useful in constructing palindromes. There are a handful of palindromic names, such as Anna, Aviva, Otto, and Hannah, but more likely your name will be featured in a palindromic statement such as *Dennis and Edna sinned.* Perhaps you or someone sharing your moniker is a participant in the following catalogue entitled "The Orgy," penned by Clement Wood.

Di, Al, Togo, Boll, Edna, Todd, Adolf, Sir Obadiah Turner, Ollie, Nora, El, silly Rama, Yma Sumac, St. Toby, Cal, Mike, Graf Alfie, Leila, Roz, Owen, Gallos, Reg, Nina Noyes, Mary, Lionel, Lana, Essex, Rex, Dr. Olim, Sal, Isobel, Ed, Axel, Ann, Odile, Leon, Bill (a Pole), Ginger, gay Ogden MacColl, Ewen, Enid, Ansel Gore, Lady Block, Cindy, Sam, Ronny, Llewellyn, Norma, Syd, Nick Colby, Dale, Rog, Les, Nadine Newell,

Occam, Ned, Goya, Greg, Nigel, Opal, Lib, Noel, Eli, Donna, Lex, Adele, Bo, Silas, Milord Xerxes, Sean Allen, oily Ramsey, Onan, Ingersoll, Agnew, Oz, Oralie, Leif LaFarge, Kim, Lacy, Botts, Camus, Amy, Amaryllis, Lear, O'Neill, Oren, Ruth, Aida, Boris, Flo, Dad, Dot, and El Lobo got laid.

First names and last names combined that are palindromic are rare, and those that do exist tend to be shortish, such as those of former leaders of Cambodia and Burma Lon Nol and U Nu. There used to be a well-known classics professor at the University of Illinois named Revilo P. Oliver. His father and grandfather enjoyed the same name, with the first of the Oliver trinity given the made-up name Revilo by his parents because it spelled Oliver backwards.

Palindromic place-names are also quite rare. There is the town of Adaven, Nevada, and Kanakanak in Alaska. People have used place-names to give their commercial establishments palindromic names, like the Yreka Bakery in Yreka, California.

Many commercial products contain palindromic names. In the case of the car Civic, the magazine *Elle*, and the deodorant named Mum, this palindromic property would appear to be accidental. I suspect, however, that products such as the silver polish Noxon, the cosmetics line Aziza, the sedative Xanax, and the baking soda Pizzazzip were chosen precisely because of their reversibility.

It is common for books about palindromes to have titles that read palindromically. The best title of this ilk, I believe, is Michael Donner's *I Love Me, Vol. I.*

The longest palindromic word in the English language is *kinnikinnik*, which is a mixture of the inner bark of dogwood and willow or dried sumac leaves, smoked by North American Indians. Although this word won't be found in every dictionary, it is listed in both *Websters' Third New International Dictionary* and *The Oxford English Dictionary*. The best effort of English, however, is dwarfed by the Finnish nineteen-letter palindromic masterpiece *saippuakivikauppias*, which refers to a trader of lye.

I suspect that Napoleon didn't know a palindrome from a hippodrome, and thus it's unlikely that he ever uttered *Able was I ere I saw Elba* himself. If he spouted a palindrome, here is a bevy of French ones he might have used:

Léon n'osa rêver à son Noël. (Leon didn't dare to think of his Christmas.)

À Laval, à Noël, Léona l'avala. (Leona swallowed it in Laval at Christmas.)

Et la marine va, papa, venir à Malte. (And the navy, daddy, is going to come to Malte.)

If Napoleon had proficiency in other European languages, he might have uttered the following:

German: *Bei Leid lieh stets heil die Lieb.* (In sorrow, love always lent security.)

Italian: *Eran I modi di dominare.* (These were the ways of domineering.)

Spanish: *Dabale arroz a la zorra el abad.* (The abbot gave the fox some rice.)

Portuguese: *Atai a gaiola, saloia gaiata.* (Tie the cage, naughty rustic girl.)

Dutch: *Neder sit wort, trow tis reden.* (Inferior is the word, enduring is the intellect.)

Latin: *Acide me malo, sed non desola me, medica.* (Disgustingly, I prefer myself, but do not leave me, healing woman.)

Napoleon could not have said *sane volema kara rara kamelo venas* ("a healthy wishful dear camel is coming") because it is in Esperanto, which was not invented until sixty-six years after his death.

So, as you can plainly see, the English language holds no palindromic monopoly, though I have been a participant in a cabal that has tried to perpetuate the myth of the primacy of English in this field. In my book *The Dead Sea Scroll Palindromes*, I suggested that certain biblical personages uttered the following English-language palindromes:

Noah: *Was it Ararat I saw?* (Genesis 8)
Delilah: *Semite mates reverse tame times.* (Judges 16)
Paul: *Egad, are we not an era midst its dim arena to newer adage?* (Romans 11)

The Oxford English Dictionary (OED) defines *palindrome* in a musical context as "a piece of music of which the second half is the first half in retrograde motion." Biologically, the OED states that it "refers to a palindromic sequence of nucleotides."

What does this mean?

A palindrome, in essence, refers to any sequence that can be read in reverse order. If there is an odd number of units, they will be arranged A-B-C-D-C-B-A, and if there is an even number of units they will have the structure A-B-C-D-D-C-B-A. Thus, the last palindromic year was 1991 and the next palindromic year will be 2002.

Palindromes can be word units as well as letter units. Probably the best known word-unit palindrome is the one associated with the Three Musketeers: *All for one and one for all.*

Many excellent word-unit palindromes were coined in the 1940s and 1950s by wordsmith J. A. Lindon. Here's a selection:

Girl, bathing on Bikini, eyeing boy, finds boy eyeing bikini on bathing-girl.
King, are you glad you are king?
So patient a doctor to doctor a patient so.
Company of fond people irks people fond of company.

Will Shortz, in his weekly puzzle segment on National Public Radio in the United States, recently held a word-unit palindrome competition. Some of the entries were *Fall leaves after leaves fall*; *Will my love love my will?*; *Blessed are they that believe that they are blessed*; and (the winning entry) *First Ladies rule the state, and state the rule — "Ladies First!"*

Readers are asked to discern the following letter-unit palindromic phrases with the clues I'm providing. When the puzzles are completed, the third letters of Puzzle A will spell out a "palindromic" language, and the second letters of Puzzle B will spell out the name of the female winner of the 1996 New York Marathon.

Puzzle A

1) Middle East newspaper?   S _ _ _ _ _   _ _ _ _ s

2) wound flying mammals   s _ _ _   _ _ _ s

3) aggressive tennis shot   b _ _ _   _ _ b

4) polygraph?   l _ _ _   _ _ _ _ l

5) Inuit canoe   k _ _ _ k

6) piece of acrobatic gear   t _ _ _ _ _ _   _ _ _ t

7) opposite of pull down?   p _ _ _ _ p

8) Persian Gulf monarchs   s _ _ _ s

9) Alaskan devil   N _ _ _ _ _ _ _ n

Puzzle B

1) Ivy League school had a race   Y _ _ _ _ _ _ _ _ _ _ _ y

2) supporters of screw-ups   s _ _ _ _ _ _ _ s

3) Maharishi's toupee?   g _ _ _ _ _ g

4) S.P.C.A. dictum?   s _ _ _ _ _ _ _ _ _ _ _ s

5) superintendent selector   n _ _ _ _ _ _ _ _ _ _ _ _ n

6) circus performers attack killer whale   a _ _ _ _ _ _ _ _ _ _ _ _ _ _ a

7) scold a fibber   r _ _ _ _ _ a _ _ _ r

8) super funny stuff by Clinton associates   s _ _ _ _ _ _ _ _ _ _ _ _ _ _ _ _ _ _ s

9) students make a mistake   p _ _ _ _ _ _ _ _ _ _ _ _ _ p

10) African antelope's refuse   g _ _ _ _ _ g

11) Mom is as generous of spirit as me   M _ _ _ _ _ _ _ _ _ _ _ _ _ _ _ _ _ m

(*Answers can be found on pages 206–7.*)

42

Definitions depend on how you split 'em

*P*eople who enjoy cryptic crossword puzzles will sometimes encounter "punnish" clues, such as "communicate devilish skill" (6 letters) or "priestly vows" (9 letters). The answers to these clues could be *impart* (*imp-art*) and *vicarious* (*vicar-ious*).

Though we think of these word tricks as puns, they aren't, in the truest sense. Punnery is primarily the trick of compacting two or more ideas within a single word or expression. Thus the pun "Have you heard about the cannibal who had a wife and ate children?" is dependent on *ate* and *eight* being homophones (i.e., that they sound alike). Puns are dependent on the sounds of words, while the essential quality in these cryptic crossword clues is not sound but spelling.

I have dubbed these word definitions *split-definitives*, because words are actually split and then defined by their constituent parts. Thus, *romantic* is defined as "centurion's twitch" and *Hebrew* is rendered as "beer with balls," because the former word can be divided into *Roman* and *tic* and the latter can be divided into *he* and *brew*.

Prefixes and suffixes, which have prescribed meanings, can also be used to form these definitions. Thus, *prediction* can be defined as "baby talk" (*pre* and *diction*).

In an article on split-definitives written for Montrealers, I probably committed a more heinous affront when I defined French words as if their constituent parts were English. Thus, *maintenant* ("now") was anglicized as "St. Lawrence Boulevard resident," because it can be divided into *Main* (the nickname for St. Lawrence Boulevard) and *tenant*; and *fartage* ("the waxing of skis") was corrupted as "natural gas production" because it broke up into *fart* and *age*. Another variation of this heresy is defining part of a word in French and part in English. In this manner, *lagoon* comes to mean "dirtiest player on a woman's hockey team," *marathon* becomes "taint a tuna," and *hambourgeoise* turned into "capitalist pig."

Many types of animals work well as split-definitives. Readers are asked to divine the following split-definitive animals by means of my cryptic clues. Each answer will feature a type of animal as one of the "definitives." Thus the clue "the first insect" (7 letters) would render the answer *adamant*. An added clue is that answers from 1 through 16 read alphabetically.

1) insect hallucinogen (7 letters)
2) constriction (8 letters)
3) sleeping bovine (10 letters)
4) rooster extremity (8 letters)
5) watering hole for the birds (7 letters)
6) bitch of a mother (5 letters)
7) pooch that scoops its own poop (8 letters)
8) pack animal (8 letters)
9) barbecued chicken (7 letters)
10) school for fat people (11 letters)

11) foreign insect (9 letters)
12) sleeping baby goat (10 letters)
13) top cat (9 letters)
14) lady horse of the evening (9 letters)
15) German prison bug (10 letters)
16) great hooter (9 letters)

(*Answers can be found on page 207.*)

43

Space: The lost frontier of wordplay

*M*ax Hall, in *An Embarrass-ment of Misprints*, relates how improper word spacing can bring about extreme journalistic embarrassment. He tells us about a headline in an unnamed American newspaper concerning a governor who had to sign a plethora of bills at the close of a legislative session. The headline was supposed to read as follows:

GOVERNOR'S PEN IS BUSY OVER WEEKEND

What the governor was busy doing seemed rather Clintonesque, however, when the headline lacked spacing between the words:

GOVERNOR'SPENISBUSYOVERWEEKEND

In the previous chapter, I discussed "split-definitives," words that are split and then redefined by their constituent parts. Take the word *malefactor*, which means "evildoer." If one creates a space between the fourth and fifth letters of *malefactor* it yields two words, *male* and *factor*, and it can now be defined as "Y chromosome."

Closely associated with "split-definitives" are what have sometimes been referred to as *charades*. Charades are a species of anagrams because they utilize the same letter stock as do anagrams. But in a charade, a word acquires a different sense solely because the spacing of the letters has been altered. For example, *therapist* and *manslaughter* are raped and slaughtered respectively when they are rendered as *the rapist* and *man's laughter*.

Here are a dozen other charades:

ass as sin	*in sect*	*redo Lent*
at ten, dance	*man ager*	*sham rock*
fat ally	*man I cure*	*stand of fish*
imp ale	*mend a city*	*war's hip*

Charades may be longer than one word. For example, the expression *soap opera* was "charaded" into *so a pop era*, and the expression *amiable together* can be seen interrogatively as *Am I able to get her?*

The sense in a charaded expression is usually totally altered, as when *Searing sun lit island* is modified to *Sea rings unlit island*. *Catch in the message* can be remodeled as *cat chin themes, sage*, and *O, had a man developed a way* can be rendered as *Oh, Adam and Eve loped away*.

Sometimes there is more than one option in a charade. *Withal, one veiled* can become *Wit, Hal. On Eve I led* or *With a lone veil, Ed.*

Charaded expressions can be quite lengthy, as in *Significant inscription: Lying old capital lines sent, I ally on estate, men, to name's sage*, which can be re-spaced into *Sign if I can't — in script. I only in gold, cap it all in essentially one statement on a message.*

Edwin Fitzgerald made a translation of Omar Khayyam's *The Rubaiyat*, which he dubbed *The Rubaiyat of Charades and Palindromes*. Here is a medley of his charades rendered in stanzaic form:

Flamingo pale, scenting a latent shark
Flaming opalescent in gala tents — hark!

No, uncle — and auntless be, as ties deny our end.
No unclean, dauntless beasties den you rend.

O fly, rich eros — dogtrot, ski, orbit eras put in swart
Of lyric heros, dog Trotski or bite Rasputin's wart.

Hiss, caress pursuit, or astound, O roc — O cobra.
His scares spur suitor as to undo rococo bra.

The multiplicity of word meanings is a boon to English-language wordplay. In English, we employ the same word for a sensitive part of a man's trousers as we do for a winged insect and the means to locomote in the air. A *set* has distinct meanings for all these groups: collectors, actors, musicians, beauticians, and tennis players. And the words *pro* and *con* each have several meanings.

Which brings us to the theme of my puzzle. Many English words begin with the words *pro* and *con*. Readers are asked to discern all the following "split-definitive" words beginning with either *pro* or *con* with the help of the clues I'm providing. For example, the answers to "in favor of metric weights" (7 letters) and "prisoner's workbench" (9 letters) would be *program* and *constable* respectively.

1) rip-off vacation (7 letters)
2) urinalysis? (7 letters)

3) Mussolini supporter (7 letters)
4) sting operation (8 letters)
5) manhunt (8 letters)
6) anti-static (9 letters)
7) what Johnny Cochrane did during the O.J. trial? (9 letters)
8) in favor of nuclear power (9 letters)
9) against the flow (10 letters)
10) creationism (10 letters)
11) prison rebellion (10 letters)
12) in favor of the Big Bang (11 letters)
13) rehabilitation (12 letters)
14) prisoner on the way down (13 letters)
15) F- for a doctor performing abortions (13 letters)

(*Answers can be found on pages 207–8.*)

Answers

Chapter 31

1) You can't teach an old dog new tricks.
2) You can't judge a book by its cover.
3) Two heads are better than one.
4) Too many cooks spoil the broth.
5) Out of sight, out of mind.
6) Actions speak louder than words.
7) There's no fool like an old fool.
8) Spare the rod and spoil the child

Chapter 39

1) acts-Cats-cast
2) Levis-Elvis-lives
3) Salem-males-meals
4) Socred-scored-credos
5) streak-skater-takers
6) lament-mantle-mental

7) trashed-threads-hardest

8) reserve-severer-reverse

9) medical-claimed-decimal

10) editors-storied-steroid

11) reduces-rescued-secured

12) optical-topical-Capitol

13) praised-aspired-diapers

14) prenatal-paternal-parental

15) alerting-integral-altering

16) thickest-thickets-thickset

17) emigrants-streaming-mastering

18) cautioned-auctioned-education

19) Sergeants-greatness-estranges

Chapter 41
A)
1) Semite Times

2) stab bats

3) bold lob

4) liar trail

5) kayak

6) trapeze part

7) pull up

8) shahs

9) Nome demon

Palindromic language: Mayalayam

B)
1) Yale ran a relay

2) snafu fans

3) guru rug

4) step not on pets

5) namer of foreman

6) acrobats stab orca

7) rail at a liar
8) star comedy by Democrats
9) pupils did slip up
10) gnu dung
11) ma is as selfless as I am

Marathon winner: Anuta Catuna

Chapter 42

1) antacid
2) boasting
3) bulldozing
4) cocktail
5) crowbar
6) dogma
7) dogmatic
8) ganglion
9) heathen
10) hippocampus
11) important
12) kidnapping
13) medallion
14) nightmare
15) stalagmite
16) superbowl

Chapter 43

1) contour
2) protest
3) produce
4) confront
5) conquest
6) promotion
7) conjurors
8) profusion

9) concurrent
10) conscience
11) conferment
12) procreation
13) constraining
14) condescending
15) proliferating